I thank my mom for introducing me to cooking
and for igniting this extraordinary passion in me.

Stefano Romor

MW01532713

Table of Contents

A CULINARY JOURNEY THROUGH ITALY.

Embark on a mouth-watering journey across. This culinary odyssey offers more than just recipes; it's a voyage into the heart of Italian culture, showcasing the unique homemade pasta of each region. From the sun-drenched hills of Tuscany to the bustling streets of Naples, each chapter unfolds the secrets behind Italy's most cherished pasta dishes.

As you turn the pages, you'll delve into the rich histories, the local anecdotes, and the artisanal traditions that make each pasta type a reflection of its homeland. Stunning photography captures the essence of these locales, while step-by-step instructions guide you in recreating these culinary masterpieces in your own kitchen.

Whether you're a seasoned chef or a passionate foodie, Pasta Tour of Italy offers a taste of Italy like never before. Discover the rustic simplicity of Puglia's orecchiette, the delicate flavors of Lombardy's pizzoccheri, and the robust heartiness of Sicilian busiate. Each recipe is more than a dish; it's a story of family, tradition, and the love of good food.

Join us on this journey and savor the true essence of Italian pasta, one region at a time.

PACK YOUR BAGS WE ARE LEAVING!

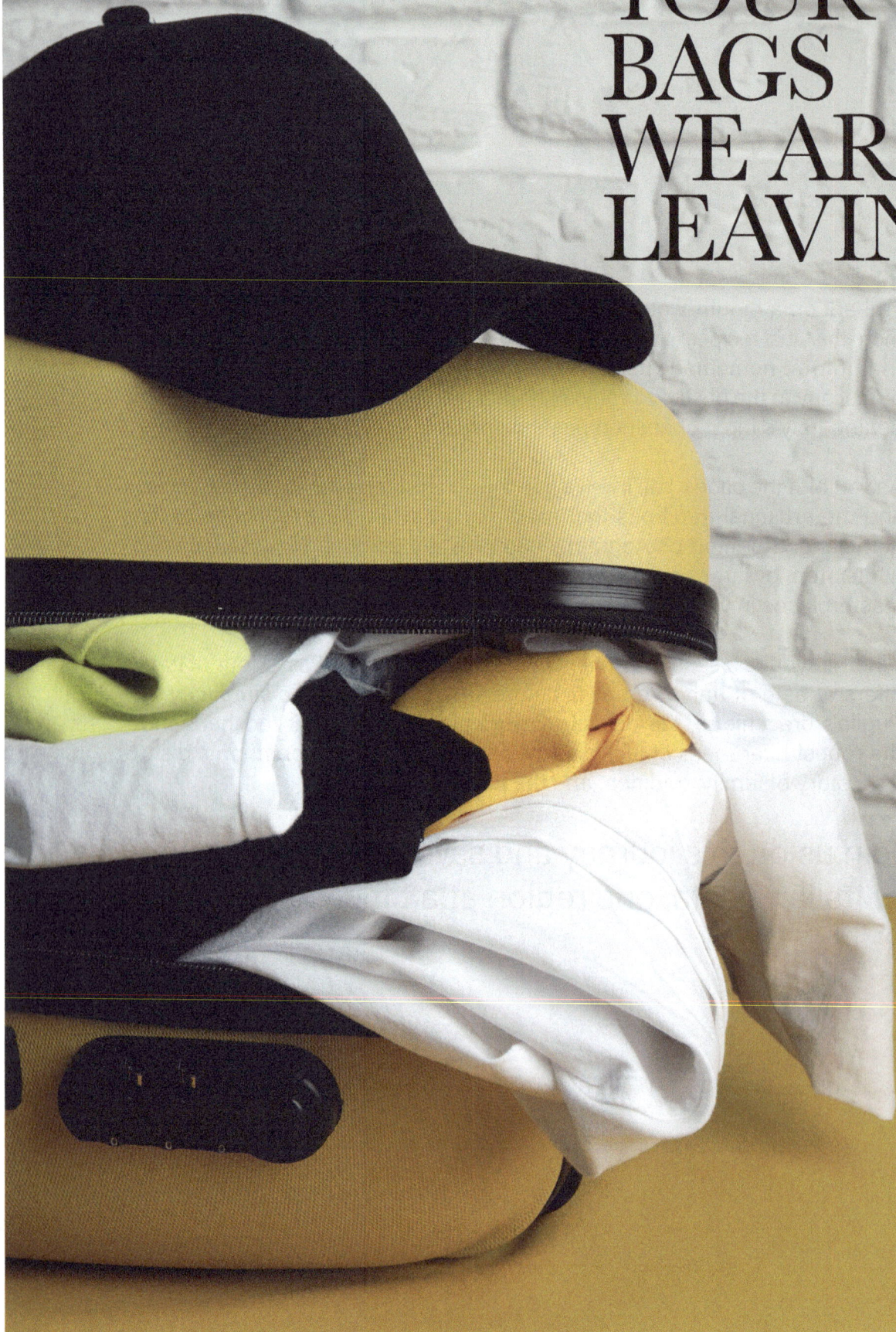

My idea is to have you take a trip through Italy, from north to south, spending a week in each of its regions and letting you discover the fresh pasta that you can taste in each one.

Italy, a country renowned for its profound beauty, offers an unparalleled tapestry of landscapes, art, history, and culture. This allure is spread across its length, from the Alpine borders in the north to the sun-kissed Mediterranean coasts in the south. The north is dominated by the majestic Alps and serene lakes like Como and Garda, providing breathtaking views and a playground for outdoor enthusiasts.

The rolling hills of Tuscany and Umbria, dotted with olive groves and vineyards, epitomize the idyllic Italian countryside.

The region's medieval towns and Renaissance cities add to its charm. The rugged beauty of the Amalfi Coast, the pristine beaches of Sardinia, and the dramatic landscapes of Sicily, with the stunning backdrop of Mount Etna, offer a more rustic and raw Italian experience. Italy is a treasure trove of art and architecture, with its roots deeply embedded in the Renaissance and Roman periods. Cities like Florence, Rome, and Venice are veritable open-air museums. The country is home to an extraordinary number of UNESCO World Heritage Sites, including the historic centers of Florence, Rome, and Venice, the Pompeii ruins, and the Baroque city of Val di Noto in Sicily.

Italians' passion for food is evident in their cuisine, which varies greatly from region to region, each boasting its own specialties and traditional dishes.

Let's not waste time and welcome aboard!

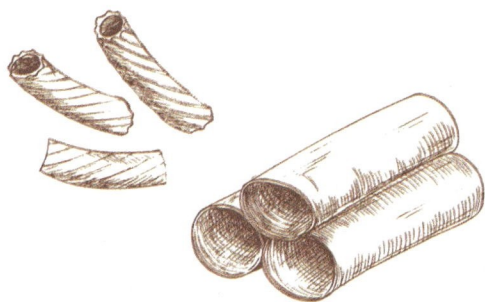

ONCE UPON A TIME THERE WAS PASTA IN ITALY.

The sfogline are the true guardians of the tradition of homemade fresh Italian pasta.

The story of homemade Italian pasta and the first "sfogline" is a rich tapestry that weaves together culinary tradition, regional variation, and artisanal craftsmanship. The term "sfoglina" (plural: "sfogline") refers to a woman who makes fresh pasta by hand, a practice deeply rooted in Italian culture, particularly in the regions of Emilia Romagna and Tuscany.

The history of pasta in Italy can be traced back to ancient times. While the exact origins are debated, it's believed that pasta was introduced to Italy during the Arab conquests of Sicily in the 8th century, or it may have been present in Etruscan and Roman diets in a different form.

Over the centuries, pasta evolved into a variety of forms across different Italian regions.

Northern Italy, with its cooler climate, was more suited to egg pasta (like tagliatelle and lasagna), while the south, with its durum wheat fields, became known for dry pasta varieties (like spaghetti and penne).

The sfogline were traditionally women who specialized in making pasta by hand. They played a crucial role in maintaining and passing down the art of pasta-making through generations. The techniques and recipes they used were often closely guarded family secrets. Making pasta by hand requires skill and patience. The sfoglina would typically roll out the pasta dough (sfoglia) with a rolling pin to a very thin consistency, which is then shaped into various forms of pasta. This hand-rolled pasta is highly prized for its texture and ability to absorb sauces. The sfogline were more than just pasta makers; they were pillars of Italian culinary culture, embodying the values of home cooking and family traditions. In many Italian households, making pasta was a communal activity, often involving multiple generations.

THE ESSENTIAL TOOLS.

To effectively stuff Italian homemade "pasta fresca" (fresh pasta), you'll need some essential equipment to streamline the process and achieve the best results. Here's a list of key tools:

1. Pasta Machine or Rolling Pin

A pasta machine is invaluable for rolling the dough to a uniform thickness. It can also be used to cut pasta into strips for certain types of stuffed pasta. Alternatively, a rolling pin can be used, though it requires more effort and skill to achieve a consistent thickness.

2. Mixing Bowls

Various sizes of mixing bowls are needed for preparing the pasta dough and the filling.

3. Sharp Knives

A good chef's knife or a sharp paring knife is essential for cutting and trimming the pasta dough.

4. Dough Scraper

A dough scraper is handy for handling and dividing the pasta dough, and also for cleaning the work surface.

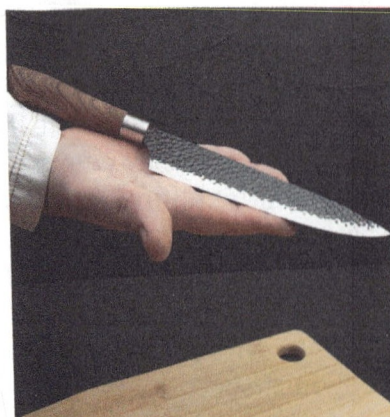

5. Ravioli Cutter or Stamp

If you're making ravioli or similar stuffed pasta, a ravioli cutter or stamp helps to cut out uniform shapes and seal the edges.

6. Fork or Pastry Wheel

A fork is useful for crimping and sealing the edges of stuffed pasta.
A pastry wheel can also be used for this purpose, especially if you want a decorative edge.

4

5

6

7

7. Piping Bags or Spoons
For filling the pasta, piping bags can be very helpful, particularly for softer, creamier fillings. Alternatively, small spoons can be used for placing the filling onto the pasta sheets.

8. Work Surface
A large, flat surface is necessary for rolling out the dough and assembling the pasta. A wooden or marble surface is ideal.

9. Cling Film or Damp Cloth
To keep the dough from drying out while you work, have some cling film or a damp cloth on hand to cover it.

Having the right equipment will make the process of making and stuffing fresh pasta much more enjoyable and efficient. Happy pasta making!

8

9

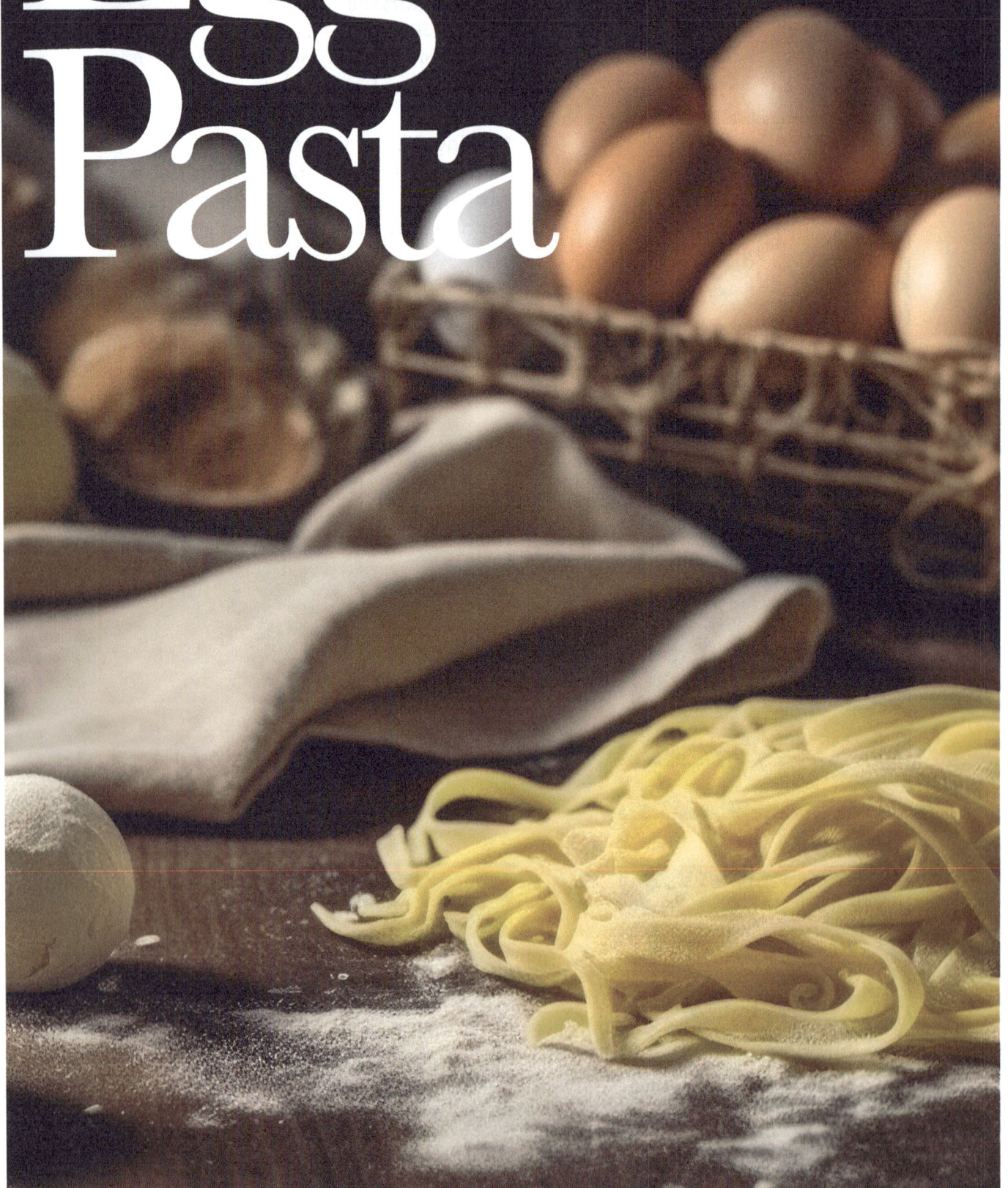

Egg Pasta

Egg pasta has its roots in the northern regions of Italy, particularly in Emilia-Romagna and Piedmont. The abundance of fresh eggs and flour in these areas led to the development of various egg pasta dishes. Famous types include tagliatelle, fettuccine, and stuffed pastas like ravioli and tortellini. Egg pasta has become a symbol of Italian home cooking and is often associated with special occasions and family gatherings. Making pasta all'uovo is a tradition passed down through generations, with recipes and techniques varying from family to family.

Stuffing homemade Italian egg pasta ("pasta all'uovo") is a delightful culinary experience. This process typically involves making a rich, pliable egg pasta dough, preparing a savory filling, and then assembling and cooking the stuffed pasta.

Ingredients
2 cups all-purpose flour (or "00" flour, if available)
3 large eggs
Pinch of salt

Instructions
On a clean surface, create a mound with the flour and form a well in the center. Crack the eggs into the well and add a pinch of salt. Gradually incorporate the flour into the eggs using a fork, combining a little at a time until a dough starts to form. Knead the dough for about 10 minutes until it becomes smooth and elastic. Wrap in plastic and let it rest for at least 30 minutes.

Semolina Pasta

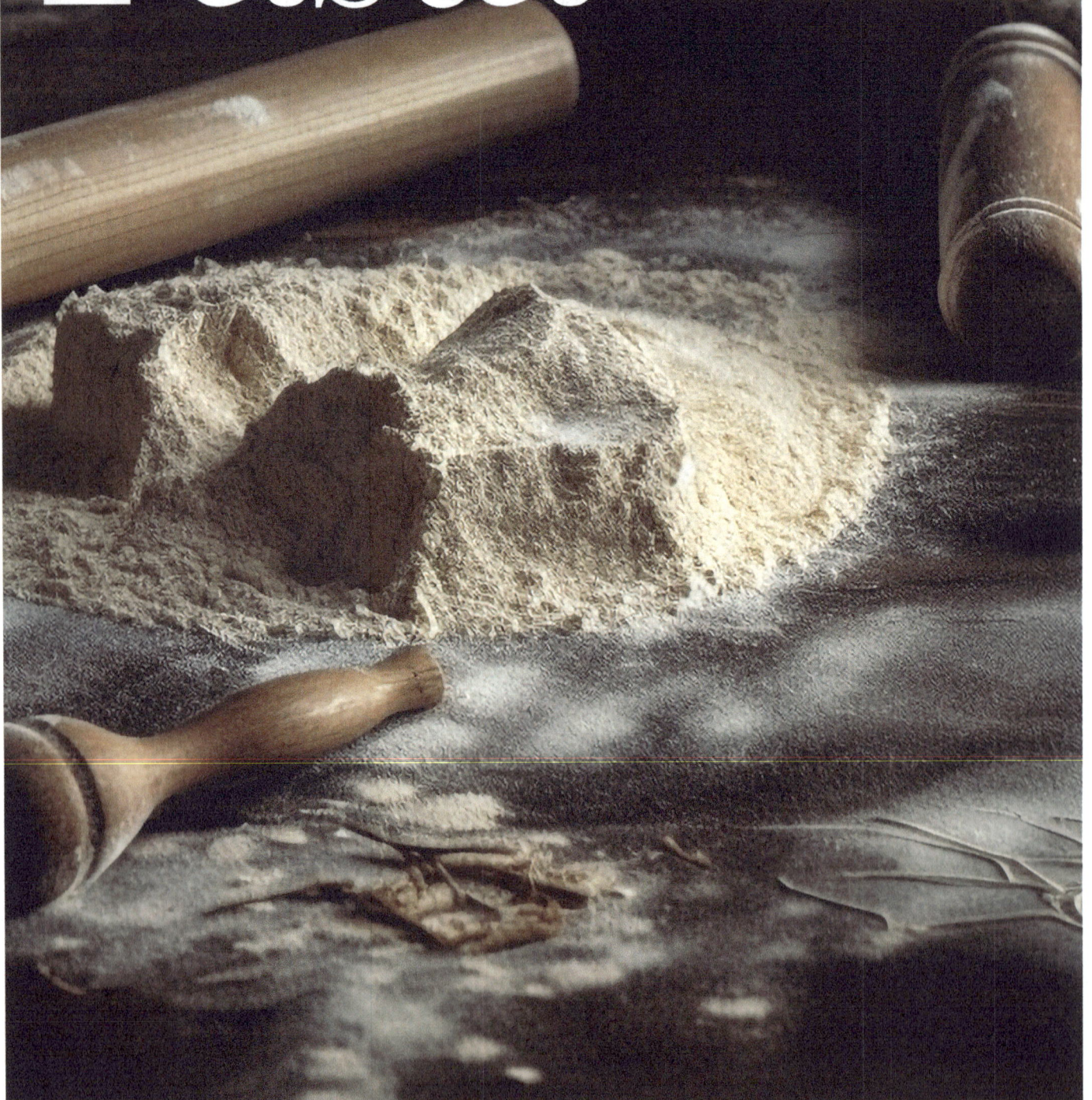

Stuffing homemade Italian semolina pasta ("pasta di semola") is a delightful culinary process, though it's important to note that traditional semolina pasta shapes, such as orecchiette or cavatelli, are typically not stuffed due to their size and structure. However, you can make larger pasta forms suitable for stuffing with semolina flour.

Ingredients
2 cups semolina flour (from durum wheat)
About 3/4 to 1 cup of water (adjust as needed)
A pinch of salt

Instructions
Mix the semolina flour and salt in a bowl. Gradually add water, stirring until a dough begins to form. You may need a little more or less water, so add it slowly.
Turn the dough out onto a floured surface and knead until smooth and elastic, about 10 minutes. Cover the dough with a damp cloth and let it rest for at least 30 minutes.

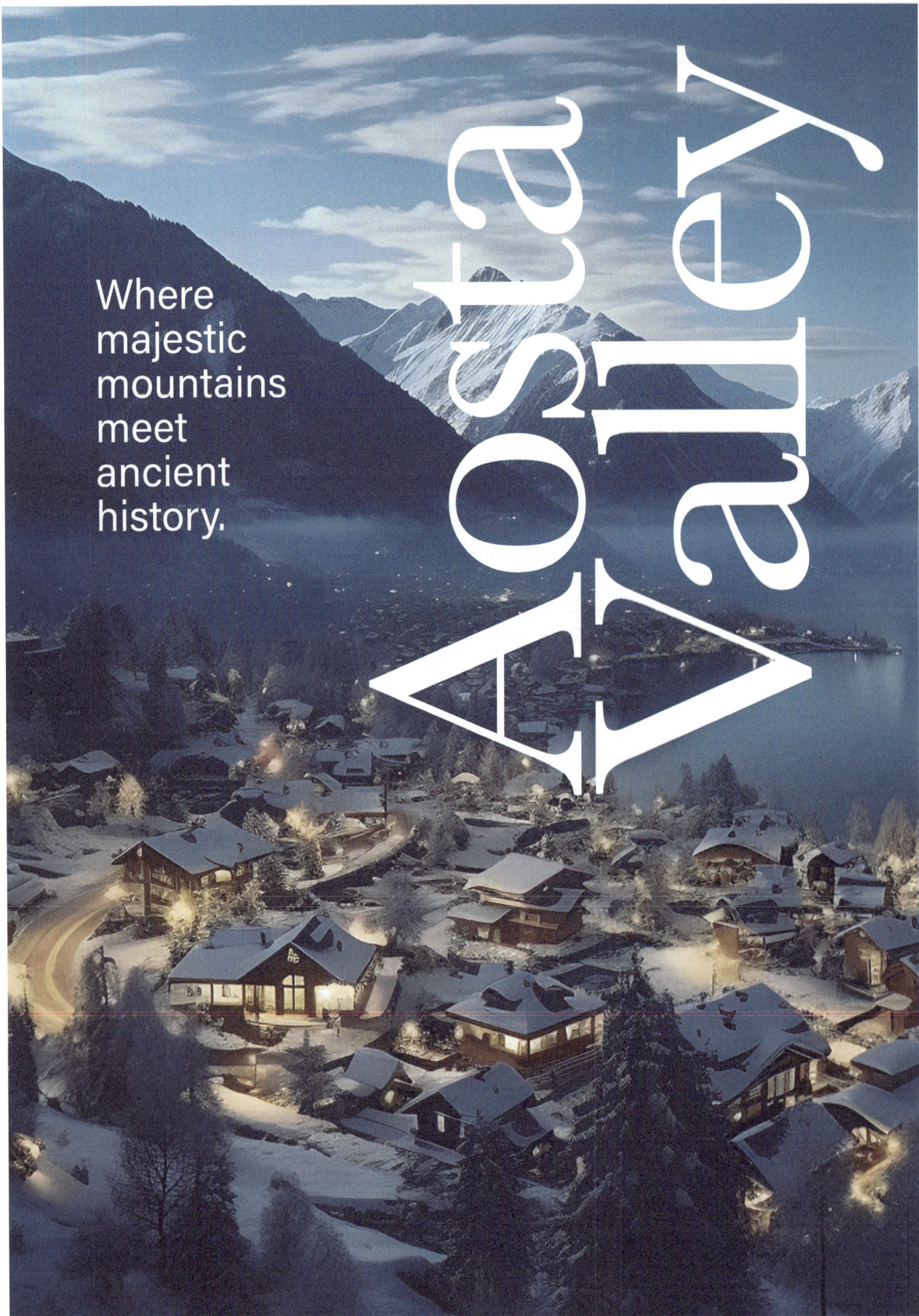

Aosta Valley

Where majestic mountains meet ancient history.

A tour of Val d'Aosta (Aosta Valley), the smallest and least populous region of Italy located in the Alps, offers a unique blend of natural beauty, ancient Roman history, and Alpine culture.

Day 1: Arrival in Aosta
Begin your journey in Aosta, the capital of the Aosta Valley. Explore the Roman ruins, including the impressive Arch of Augustus and the Roman Theatre. Visit the Aosta Cathedral and stroll through the historic center.

Day 2: Castles and Fortresses
The Aosta Valley is known for its numerous castles. Visit the Fénis Castle, one of the most famous and well-preserved medieval castles in Italy. Head to the Forte di Bard, a restored fortress that now hosts museum exhibitions and cultural events.

In the evening, enjoy traditional Valdostan cuisine, such as "polenta concia" or "carbonada."

Day 3: Mont Blanc and Courmayeur
Travel to Courmayeur, a charming town at the foot of Mont Blanc, the highest mountain in the Alps. Take the Skyway Monte Bianco, a rotating cable car, for breathtaking views of Mont Blanc and the surrounding peaks. Enjoy hiking or relax in one of the town's many cafes.

Day 4: Gran Paradiso National Park
Visit Gran Paradiso National Park, Italy's first national park, known for its stunning alpine scenery and wildlife.

Take a guided hike or nature walk to explore the park's flora and fauna. Visit the park's visitor centers to learn more about its history and environmental significance.

Day 5: Cogne and the Valnontey Valley
Head to the picturesque town of Cogne, nestled in the heart of the Gran Paradiso National Park. Explore the Valnontey Valley, known for its beautiful meadows, hiking trails, and opportunities to spot wildlife. Relax at a local spa or wellness center in the evening.

Day 6: Skiing and Winter Sports (Winter) / Hiking and Mountain Biking (Summer)
Depending on the season, enjoy the region's outdoor activities. In winter, the Aosta Valley offers excellent skiing and snowboarding. In summer, it's perfect for hiking, mountain biking, and climbing. Visit resorts like Cervinia, linked to Zermatt in Switzerland, or Pila, easily accessible from Aosta.

Day 7: Departure
Spend your last day in Aosta, perhaps doing some shopping for local products like Fontina cheese, Valdostan wine, or artisanal crafts. Depart from the Aosta Valley, either by car through the scenic mountain routes or via the nearest airport.

Homemade Pasta from Aosta Valley

The cuisine of the Aosta Valley is a mountain cuisine, given the territory surrounded by peaks.

As the smallest Italian region with its mountainous conformation, this characteristic has also influenced its dining culture. In the past, it was difficult to cultivate all the products locally and to cross the mountain borders to procure them from neighboring regions; hence, the recipes are almost entirely made with local products. For this reason, the regional cuisine lacks pasta, which is replaced by famous soups made with rice, bread, and cheese. Among the few typical pasta dishes of the Aosta Valley are the chestnut fettuccine. Historically, as mentioned, white flour was scarce and difficult to find, so alternative flours like chestnut flour were used. The dough was made with a minimal amount of soft wheat flour, salt, and water. Once the dough was made, the pasta was rolled out (as it still is today), rolled up, and cut into strips, more or less thin, like normal fettuccine.

How the Chestnut Fettuccina is Born.

In Valle d'Aosta, a region known for its stunning mountains and hearty cuisine, chestnuts have long been a staple food, especially in the colder months.

The story goes that many years ago, during a particularly harsh winter, a shortage of wheat flour led the resourceful people of the region to look for alternatives. They turned to chestnuts, which were abundant in the local forests, grinding them into flour. The chestnut flour was then used to make pasta, giving birth to Fettuccine di Castagna. This pasta was not only a creative solution to a shortage but also turned out to be deliciously unique, with a slightly sweet and earthy flavor that was different from any traditional pasta. It became a beloved winter dish, often served with rich, meaty sauces that complemented its distinct taste.

This innovative use of chestnut flour is a testament to the resilience and ingenuity of the people of Valle d'Aosta. It also reflects the region's deep connection to its natural environment, using what the land provides to create something both nourishing and enjoyable. To this day, Fettuccine di Castagna remains a symbol of Valle d'Aosta's culinary heritage, a dish born out of necessity that has become a cherished part of local cuisine.

Fettuccine di Castagne ai Funghi Porcini
Chestnut Fettuccine with Porcini Mushrooms

Ingredients

For the Fettuccine:
1 cup chestnut flour
1 cup all-purpose flour (or soft wheat flour)
2 large eggs
A pinch of salt
Water, as needed

For the Sauce:
2 cups fresh porcini mushrooms, cleaned and sliced
2 cloves of garlic, minced
1/4 cup extra virgin olive oil
1/2 cup white wine
Salt and pepper, to taste
Fresh parsley, chopped
Grated Parmesan cheese (optional)

Instructions

In a large bowl, combine the chestnut flour and all-purpose flour with a pinch of salt. Make a well in the center and add the eggs. Begin mixing the eggs with the flour, gradually adding a little water if necessary, until a dough forms. Turn the dough onto a floured surface and knead until smooth and elastic.

Wrap the dough in plastic wrap and let it rest for about 30 minutes. Roll the dough into a thin sheet, then roll it up and slice it into thin strips to create fettuccine. Unroll the strips and let them dry for a few minutes.

Preparing the Sauce:

In a large pan, heat the olive oil over medium heat. Add the minced garlic and sauté until fragrant.

Cook the Mushrooms: Add the sliced porcini mushrooms and cook until they start to soften.

Pour in the white wine and let it simmer until the alcohol evaporates.

Season with salt, pepper, and add chopped parsley.

In a large pot of salted boiling water, cook the fettuccine until al dente.

Combine with Sauce: Drain the pasta and add it to the mushroom sauce. Toss well to coat the fettuccine evenly. Serve hot, garnished with grated Parmesan cheese and additional parsley if desired.

Fettuccine di Castagne alla Bava
Chestnut Fettuccine with Creamy Cheese Sauce

Ingredients

For the Fettuccine:
1 cup chestnut flour
1 cup all-purpose flour (or soft wheat flour)
2 large eggs
A pinch of salt
Water, as needed

For the Alla Bava Sauce:
1 cup Fontina cheese, grated
1/2 cup heavy cream
2 tablespoons butter
Nutmeg, a pinch
Salt and pepper, to taste

Instructions

In a large bowl, combine the chestnut flour and all-purpose flour with a pinch of salt.

Create a well in the center and add the eggs. Gradually mix in the eggs with the flour, adding a bit of water if necessary, until a dough forms.

Knead the dough on a floured surface until it's smooth and elastic. Let the dough rest wrapped in plastic for about 30 minutes. Roll the dough into a thin sheet, then roll it up and cut into thin strips. Unroll the strips to form fettuccine and let them dry slightly.

Preparing the Alla Bava Sauce:

In a saucepan, melt the butter over medium heat.

Add Cream and Cheese: Stir in the heavy cream and then gradually add the grated Fontina cheese. Keep stirring until the cheese melts and the sauce is creamy.

Season: Add a pinch of nutmeg and season with salt and pepper to taste. Cook the fettuccine in a pot of salted boiling water until al dente.

Drain the pasta and mix it into the cheese sauce, ensuring the fettuccine is well coated.

Serve immediately, offering a comforting and decadent meal.

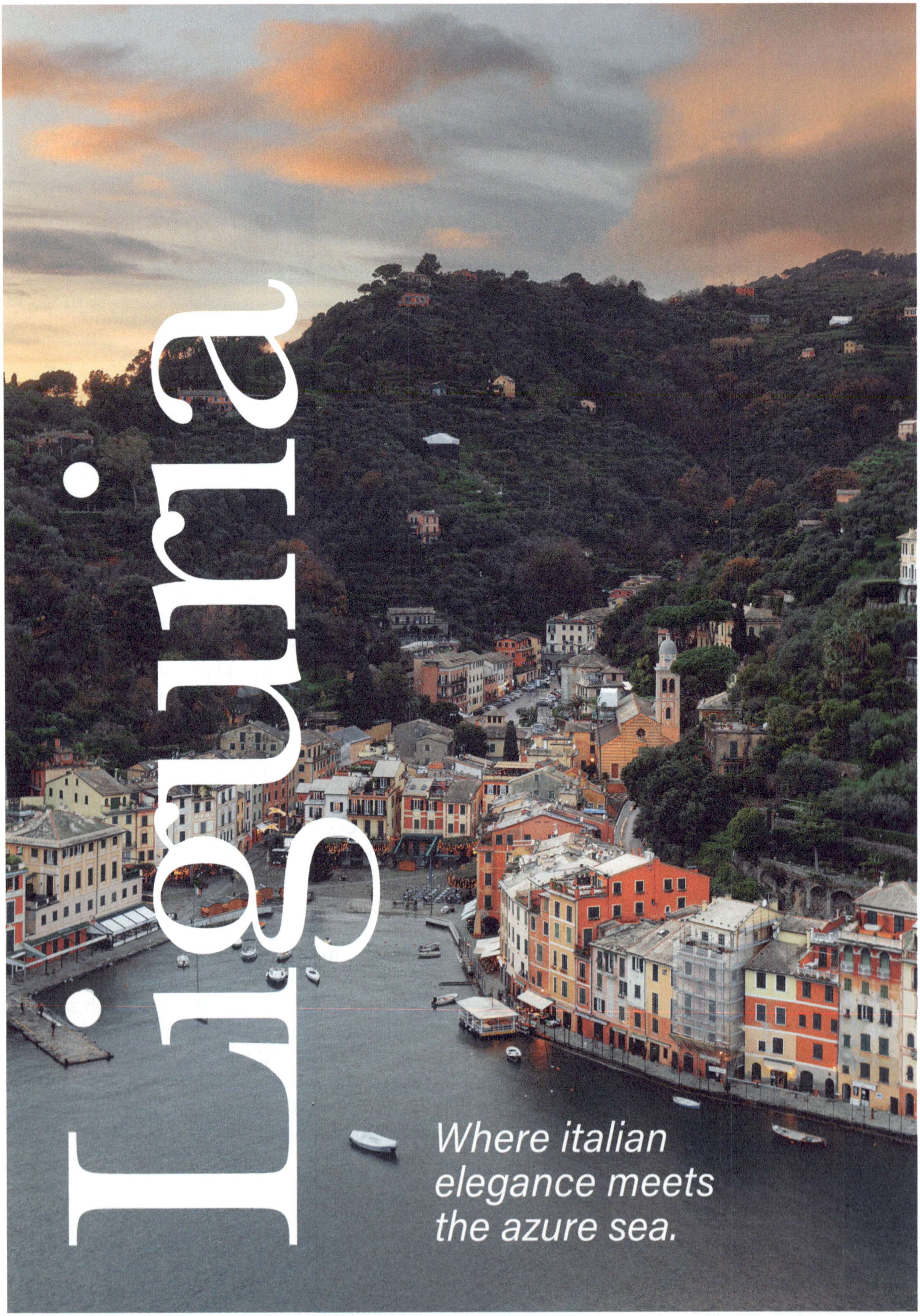

Liguria

Where italian elegance meets the azure sea.

A tour of Liguria, a coastal region in northwestern Italy, known for its picturesque landscapes, charming seaside towns, and rich culinary traditions, offers a captivating experience. Here's what a tour through Liguria might include:

Day 1: Arrival in Genoa

Start your journey in Genoa, the capital of Liguria. Explore the old town, a UNESCO World Heritage site, with its narrow lanes (caruggi) and visit the Cathedral of San Lorenzo.

See the famous aquarium, one of the largest in Europe, and stroll along the Porto Antico.

Day 2: The Cinque Terre Travel to the Cinque Terre, a string of five fishing villages perched along the rugged coastline, also a UNESCO World Heritage site.

Visit villages like Riomaggiore, Manarola, Vernazza, and Monterosso al Mare, each with its unique charm. Enjoy hiking along the coastal paths, offering stunning sea views and vineyard landscapes.

Day 3: Portovenere and the Gulf of Poets

Explore Portovenere, located at the end of the Cinque Terre coastline, known for its picturesque harbor and the Church of San Pietro.

Take a boat trip around the Gulf of Poets, so named for the poets like Byron and Shelley who were inspired by its beauty. Enjoy seafood cuisine, with dishes featuring fresh local fish and Ligurian olive oil.

Day 4: Portofino and Santa Margherita Ligure

Visit the glamorous town of Portofino, famous for its colorful houses and luxury yachts. Spend some time in Santa Margherita Ligure, a charming seaside town with lovely beaches and a relaxed atmosphere. Explore the Abbey of San Fruttuoso, accessible by hiking or boat, with its beautiful beach and clear waters.

Day 5: The Riviera di Levante

Head to the Riviera di Levante, visiting towns like Sestri Levante and Chiavari. Enjoy the beaches and explore the historical centers of these lesser-known but equally charming towns. Sample local specialties like focaccia, farinata, and pesto, a Ligurian creation.

Day 6: The Riviera di Ponente

Explore the Riviera di Ponente, visiting places like Finale Ligure, Alassio, and the medieval village of Cervo.

Enjoy the sandy beaches and the lively atmosphere of these coastal towns. Visit the gardens of Villa Hanbury near Ventimiglia, near the French border.

Day 7: Departure from Genoa

Spend your last day in Genoa, perhaps visiting the Palazzi dei Rolli, a series of elegant residences that are part of the city's UNESCO heritage. Enjoy a final stroll along the city's ancient walls or a visit to the bustling markets for last-minute souvenirs. Depart from Genoa's international airport or train station.

Trofie

Homemade pasta from Liguria

Homemade pasta from Liguria, a coastal region in northwestern Italy, reflects the area's rich culinary traditions and its bountiful natural resources.

Ligurian pasta is known for its simplicity, fresh ingredients, and unique shapes.

Trofie: One of the most iconic Ligurian pasta shapes. Trofie are small, twisted pieces of pasta made from flour and water. They are often served with pesto, the famous sauce originating from Genoa, made with basil, pine nuts, garlic, Parmesan cheese, Pecorino cheese, and olive oil.

Pansotti: Similar to ravioli, pansotti are stuffed pasta typically filled with a mixture of several greens (like spinach, chard, and others), ricotta cheese, and sometimes herbs. They are often served with a walnut sauce, another Ligurian specialty.

Corzetti or Croxetti: These are unique, coin-shaped pasta discs that are stamped with intricate designs. The designs are traditionally made using wooden stamps and can include family crests or other motifs. Corzetti is typically served with pesto or a mushroom sauce.

Taglierini: A thin, ribbon-like pasta similar to tagliatelle but narrower. It's often served with light sauces, seafood, or incorporated into soup dishes.

Trenette: A type of narrow, flat pasta similar to linguine. Trenette is traditionally served with pesto, potatoes, and green beans, creating a hearty and flavorful dish.

The pesto is the quintessential ligurian condiment and accompanies all homemade pastas.

Ingredients

2 cups fresh basil leaves (preferably small, young leaves)
1/2 cup extra virgin olive oil
6 tablespoons grated Parmigiano-Reggiano cheese
2 tablespoons grated Pecorino cheese
1/3 cup pine nuts
2 garlic cloves, peeled
A pinch of salt

Instructions

Gently rinse the basil leaves in cold water and pat them dry with a paper towel. It's important to be gentle to avoid bruising the leaves.

In a mortar and pestle, crush the garlic cloves with a pinch of salt until it forms a paste. Add the pine nuts and continue to crush until everything is finely ground. Gradually add the basil leaves, crushing and grinding them against the sides of the mortar. The key is to use a circular motion to release the oils and fragrance of the basil without overheating the leaves. Once the basil is reduced to a paste, stir in the Parmigiano Reggiano and Pecorino cheeses. Slowly drizzle in the olive oil, continuing to mix and crush the ingredients until you achieve a smooth, emulsified sauce.

If the pesto is too thick, add a little more olive oil until you reach the desired consistency. Taste the pesto and adjust the seasoning, adding more salt or cheese if needed.

A DIVE INTO THE PAST

The Origin of Trofie

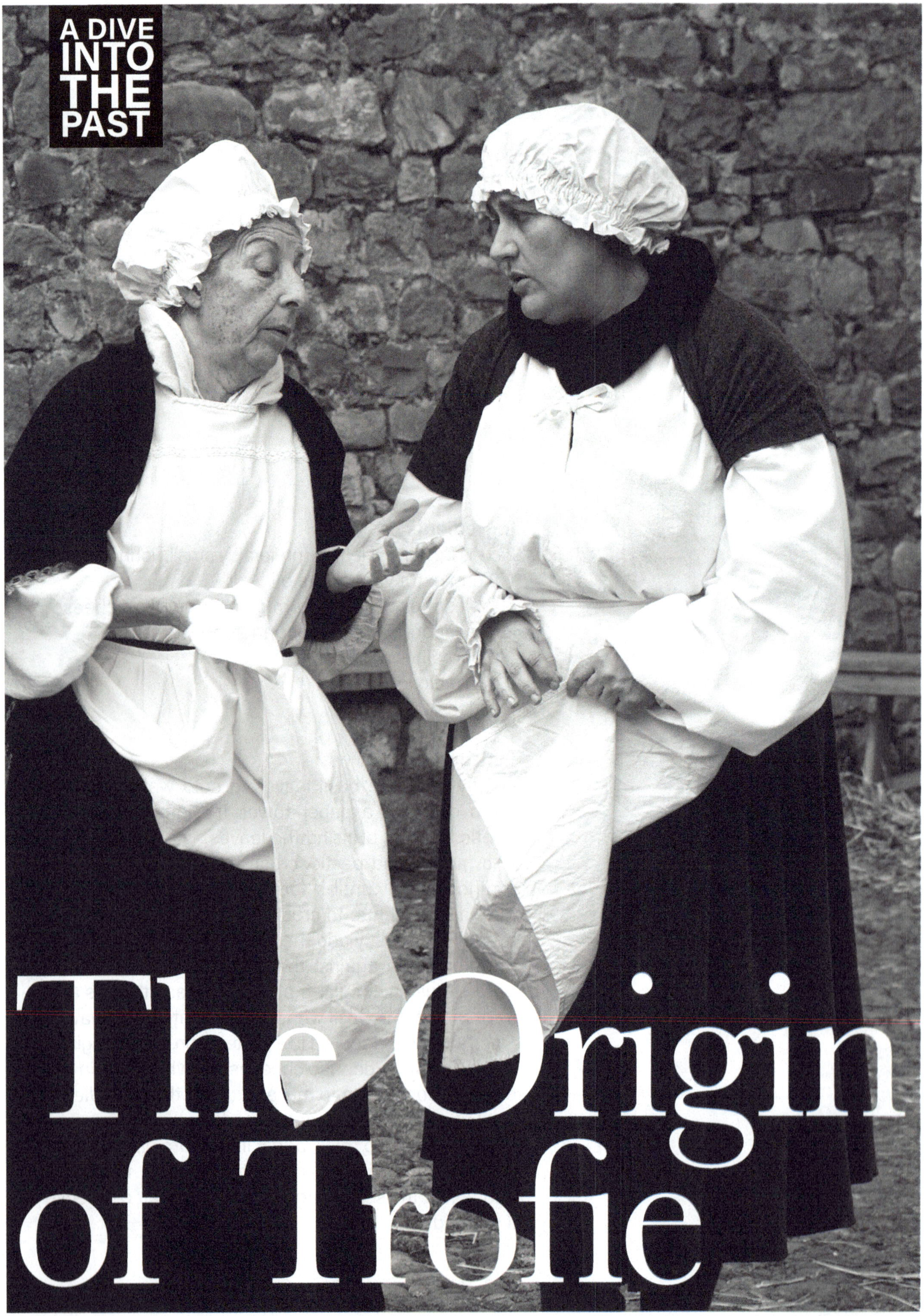

One charming anecdote about Trofie, the traditional pasta from Liguria, Italy, revolves around its humble origins and unique shape. Trofie is known for its small, twisted form, which is achieved by rolling small pieces of pasta dough by hand.

The story goes that Trofie was born out of the creativity and resourcefulness of Ligurian housewives. In the past, women in the coastal villages of Liguria would often gather to make pasta together. They wanted to create a pasta shape that didn't require any special equipment, something that could be easily made by hand while chatting and sharing stories.

The women experimented with different techniques and eventually discovered that by rolling a small piece of dough against the surface of a table or board with the palm of their hand, they could create a shape that was not only beautiful but also practical. The twisted shape of Trofie allowed it to hold onto sauces better, making it a perfect match for the famous pesto alla Genovese, a sauce also native to Liguria.

Over time, Trofie became a staple in Ligurian cuisine, often served during gatherings and celebrations.

It symbolizes the simplicity and ingenuity of traditional Italian cooking, where a few basic ingredients and a little creativity can give birth to a dish that is both delicious and deeply rooted in the culture and community of its origin.

Trofie al Pesto
Trofie with Pesto Sauce

Ingredients
For the Trofie:
2 cups all-purpose flour (or 00 flour, if available)
3/4 cup warm water
A pinch of salt
For the Pesto:
See page 33

Instructions
Place the flour in a mound on a clean surface or in a large bowl. Make a well in the center.
Gradually add warm water to the well, mixing it with the flour using your hands or a fork.
Add a pinch of salt. Knead the dough for about 10 minutes, until it's smooth and elastic. If the dough is too sticky, add a bit more flour; if it's too dry, add a little more water. Wrap the dough in plastic wrap or cover it with an inverted bowl and let it rest for about 30 minutes. This resting period allows the gluten in the dough to relax, making it easier to shape.
Cut a small portion of the dough and roll it into a thin rope, about 1/4 inch in diameter. Keep the rest of the dough covered to prevent it from drying out. Cut the rope into small pieces, about 1 inch long. Using the palm of your hand, roll each piece on the work surface, pressing down slightly and moving your hand towards you to create a twisted, elongated shape. The traditional trofie shape resembles a small, twisted spiral or a curl. Bring a large pot of salted water to a boil. Add the trofie and cook for about 2-3 minutes, or until they float to the surface and are al dente. Drain the pasta and combine it with your sauce of choice, such as a traditional pesto.

Lasagne al Pesto
Lasagne with Pesto Sauce

Ingredients

For the Fresh Pasta:
3 cups all-purpose flour,
plus extra for dusting
4 large eggs
1 tablespoon olive oil
A pinch of salt
For the Pesto:
See page 33
For the Bechamel Sauce:
4 cups milk
1/2 cup butter
1/2 cup all-purpose flour
A pinch of nutmeg
Salt and pepper to taste
Additional Ingredients:
1 cup grated Parmesan cheese
1 cup ricotta cheese (optional)

Instructions

Place the flour in a mound on a flat surface. Make a well in the center and crack in the eggs. Add the olive oil and salt. Gradually mix the flour into the eggs using a fork until the mixture becomes thick.

Knead the dough with your hands for about 10 minutes until it becomes smooth and elastic. Add more flour if the dough is too sticky. Wrap the dough in plastic wrap and let it rest for about 30 minutes.

Divide the dough into smaller portions. Flatten each portion with a rolling pin or use a pasta machine to roll the dough into thin sheets, about the thickness of a dime.Cut the sheets into lasagna-sized strips (usually about 4 inches wide). Let them dry slightly on a floured surface. In a saucepan, melt the butter over medium heat. Add flour and stir until the mixture becomes pale golden. Gradually whisk in the milk to avoid lumps. Cook until the sauce thickens. Season with nutmeg, salt, and pepper. Preheat the oven to 375°F (190°C). Have your pesto, bechamel sauce, grated Parmesan, and ricotta (if using) ready. Spread a thin layer of bechamel sauce in the bottom of a baking dish. Place a layer of pasta sheets over the sauce. Spread a layer of pesto over the pasta, followed by dollops of ricotta (if using), and then a layer of bechamel sauce. Sprinkle with grated Parmesan. Repeat the layers until all ingredients are used, finishing with bechamel and Parmesan on top. Cover with foil and bake for about 25 minutes. Then remove the foil and bake for an additional 10-15 minutes until the top is golden and bubbly. Allow the lasagna to rest for a few minutes before serving. This helps the layers set, making it easier to cut and serve.

Pansotti
a traditional stuffed pasta similar to ravioli or tortelloni, typically filled with a mixture of greens and cheese.

Ingredients
2 cups all-purpose flour
2 large eggs
1 tablespoon olive oil
Water, as needed
A pinch of salt
For the Filling:
2 cups mixed greens (such as spinach, chard, and wild greens)
1 cup ricotta cheese
1/2 cup grated Parmesan cheese
1 egg
Nutmeg, to taste
Salt and pepper, to taste

Instructions
On a clean surface, make a mound out of the flour and form a well in the center. Crack the eggs into the well, add olive oil and a pinch of salt.

Gradually incorporate the flour into the eggs and oil, mixing with your fingers. Add a little water if the dough is too dry. Knead the dough for about 10 minutes until it's smooth and elastic. Wrap in plastic wrap and let it rest for 30 minutes.

Wash the greens and cook them in boiling salted water until tender. Drain well and squeeze out excess water. Chop the greens finely.

In a bowl, combine the chopped greens, ricotta, Parmesan, egg, nutmeg, salt, and pepper. Mix until well combined. Divide the dough into smaller portions. Roll each portion into thin sheets using a rolling pin or a pasta machine.

Place small spoonfuls of filling about 1 inch apart on one sheet of pasta. Cover with another sheet of pasta. Press down around the filling to seal and remove air pockets.

Cut into individual pansotti using a pasta cutter or knife. Make sure the edges are well sealed.

Bring a large pot of salted water to a boil. Cook the pansotti in batches for about 3-4 minutes or until they float to the top. Remove with a slotted spoon and drain.

Pansotti con Salsa di Noci
Pansotti with Walnut Sauce

Ingredients
For the Pansotti Filling and the Pasta Dough:
See page 37
For the Salsa di Noci (Walnut Sauce):
1 cup walnuts
1/2 cup milk or heavy cream
1 small garlic clove
1/2 cup grated Parmesan cheese
2-3 tablespoons olive oil
Salt and pepper, to taste
A pinch of nutmeg

Instructions
Making the Pansotti:
See page 33
Preparing the Salsa di Noci:
Soak the walnuts in milk or cream for about an hour, then blend with garlic, Parmesan, and olive oil.
Season with nutmeg, salt, and pepper.
Cook the Pansotti: boil the pansotti in salted water until they float to the surface, then drain. Toss the pansotti gently with the walnut sauce and serve.

Corzetti
also known as croxetti. These are small, round pasta discs often embossed with decorative patterns.

Ingredients
2 cups all-purpose flour
(or a mix of all-purpose and semolina flour for extra texture)
2 large eggs
A pinch of salt
Water, as needed
Equipment:
Corzetti stamp (optional, but traditionally used to create the decorative patterns)
Round cookie cutter or a small glass

Instructions
Place the flour on a clean surface and make a well in the center. Crack the eggs into the well and add a pinch of salt. Gradually mix the flour into the eggs using a fork or your fingers. If the dough is too dry, add a little water, a teaspoon at a time, until it comes together.

Knead the dough for about 8-10 minutes until it's smooth and elastic. Wrap in plastic wrap and let it rest for about 30 minutes. Divide the dough into smaller portions for easier handling. Roll out one portion at a time on a floured surface to about 1/8 inch thickness. Keep the rest of the dough covered to prevent it from drying out.

Using a round cookie cutter or a small glass, cut out circles from the rolled dough.

If you have a corzetti stamp, press it onto each circle to emboss the decorative pattern. If you don't have a stamp, you can use a fork to create a simple pattern.

Bring a large pot of salted water to a boil.

Gently add the corzetti and cook for about 2-3 minutes or until they float to the surface.

Drain and serve with your sauce of choice.

Corzetti pairs well with traditional pesto, walnut sauce, or a simple butter and sage sauce.

Taglierini
similar to tagliatelle but thinner.

Ingredients
2 cups all-purpose flour
(or a mix of all-purpose and semolina
flour for extra texture)
3 large eggs
1 tablespoon olive oil
A pinch of salt
Water, as needed (if the dough is too dry)

Instructions
On a clean surface, create a mound with the flour and form a well in the center. Crack the eggs into the well, add the olive oil and a pinch of salt.

Gradually mix the flour into the eggs and oil, using your fingers or a fork, until a dough starts to form. If it's too dry, add a little water.

Knead the dough for about 10 minutes until it becomes smooth and elastic. The dough should be firm but pliable. If it's sticky, add a bit more flour.

Wrap the dough in plastic wrap and let it rest for about 30 minutes at room temperature. This resting period allows the gluten in the dough to relax, making it easier to roll out. Divide the dough into smaller portions for easier handling. Roll out each portion on a floured surface. Start from the center of the dough and roll outward. Keep turning the dough and rolling until it's very thin, almost transparent (ideally about 1/16 inch thick).

You can also use a pasta machine to roll the dough to the desired thickness.

Once the dough is rolled out, let it dry slightly for a few minutes. Then, fold it loosely into a flat roll.

Using a sharp knife, cut thin strips (about 1/8 inch wide) from the roll.

Unravel the strips and dust them lightly with flour to prevent sticking. Bring a large pot of salted water to a boil. Add the taglierini and cook for 2-3 minutes or until al dente. Drain the pasta, reserving a little of the cooking water to adjust the sauce consistency if needed.

Taglierini pairs well with light, delicate sauces like a simple tomato sauce, pesto, or even just butter and Parmesan cheese.

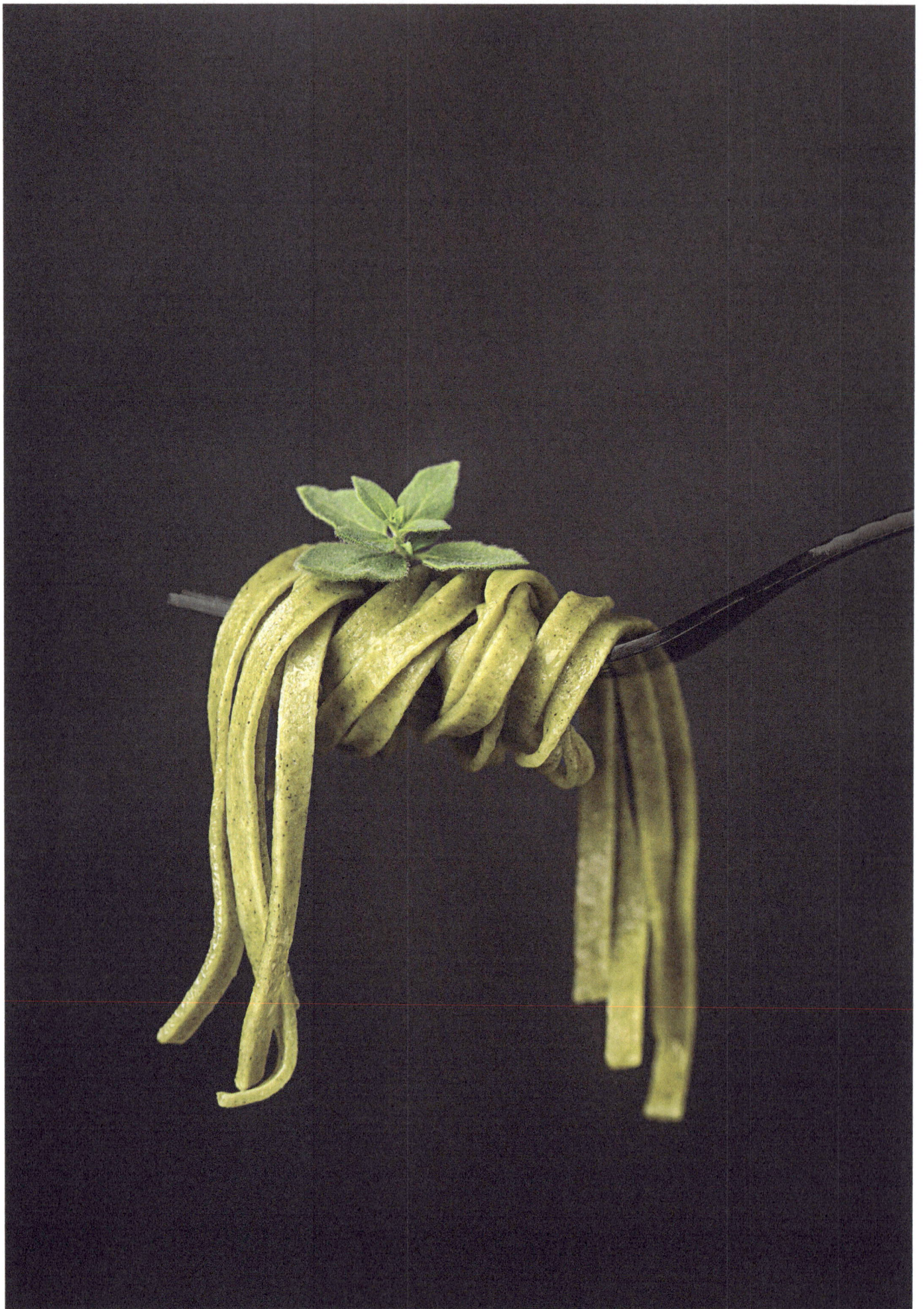

Trenette

similar to linguine but slightly flatter and narrower, is a classic dish often served with pesto, potatoes and green beans.

Ingredients

2 cups all-purpose flour (or a mix of all-purpose and semolina flour for extra texture)
3 large eggs
1 tablespoon olive oil
A pinch of salt
Water, as needed (if the dough is too dry)

Instructions

On a clean surface, make a mound of flour and create a well in the center.

Crack the eggs into the well, add the olive oil, and a pinch of salt. Gradually incorporate the flour into the egg mixture using a fork or your fingers. If the dough feels too dry, add a little water to achieve the right consistency.

Knead the dough for about 10 minutes until it becomes smooth and elastic. The dough should be firm but not too sticky. Add a bit more flour if necessary.

Wrap the dough in plastic wrap and let it rest for about 30 minutes at room temperature. This step allows the gluten in the dough to relax, making it easier to roll out.

Divide the dough into smaller portions for easier handling. Using a rolling pin or a pasta machine, roll each portion into thin sheets. The thickness should be slightly less than that of tagliatelle.

Once the dough is rolled out to the desired thickness, let it dry slightly for a few minutes.

Cut the sheets into narrow strips, about 1/4 inch wide. Dust the cut pasta with a little flour to prevent sticking.

Bring a large pot of salted water to a boil.

Cook the trenette for 2-3 minutes or until they reach the desired al dente texture.

Trenette is traditionally served with pesto sauce. You can also toss it with a light tomato sauce, olive oil and garlic, or any sauce that complements its delicate texture.

For a traditional Ligurian dish, serve trenette with pesto, boiled potatoes, and green beans.

Where timeless
heritage meets
modern splendor.

Lombardy

Lombardia (Lombardy), a region in northern Italy known for its diverse landscapes, rich history, and economic importance, offers a journey through bustling cities, serene lakes, and alpine mountains.

Day 1: Arrival in Milan

Begin your tour in Milan, the capital of Lombardy and a global fashion and design capital.

Visit the iconic Duomo di Milano, a stunning Gothic cathedral, and explore the Galleria Vittorio Emanuele II, one of the world's oldest shopping malls.

Experience the art and culture of the city, including a visit to see Leonardo da Vinci's "The Last Supper" (booking in advance is essential).

Day 2: Milan's Cultural Treasures

Spend another day in Milan exploring its many museums and galleries, such as the Pinacoteca di Brera or the Castello Sforzesco.

Stroll through the vibrant neighborhoods, like Brera or Navigli, and enjoy Milanese cuisine in a local trattoria.

Day 3: Lake Como

Travel to Lake Como, famous for its stunning landscapes and luxurious villas. Visit the charming towns of Bellagio, Varenna, and Como, enjoying boat trips on the lake. Explore Villa Carlotta or Villa del Balbianello, known for their beautiful gardens and architecture.

Day 4: Bergamo

Head to Bergamo, a city with a rich history and stunning architecture. Explore the Città Alta (Upper Town), a medieval city center surrounded by Venetian walls, and visit landmarks like the Basilica di Santa Maria Maggiore and the Campanone tower. Enjoy traditional Bergamasque cuisine, including polenta and casoncelli (stuffed pasta).

Day 5: The Franciacorta Wine Region

Visit the Franciacorta region, known for its sparkling wines.

Enjoy a wine-tasting tour, exploring vineyards and sampling the local Franciacorta DOCG.

Visit the beautiful Abbey of San Pietro in Lamosa in Provaglio d'Iseo.

Day 6: The Alps and Brescia

Spend a day in the Italian Alps, possibly visiting the Adamello Ski area or the Stelvio National Park. On the way back, stop in Brescia, known for its Roman and Lombard heritage. Visit the UNESCO listed monastery complex of San Salvatore-Santa Giulia and the Roman ruins in the city.

Day 7: Departure from Milan

Return to Milan for any final sightseeing or shopping. Depart from Milan's international airport or train station.

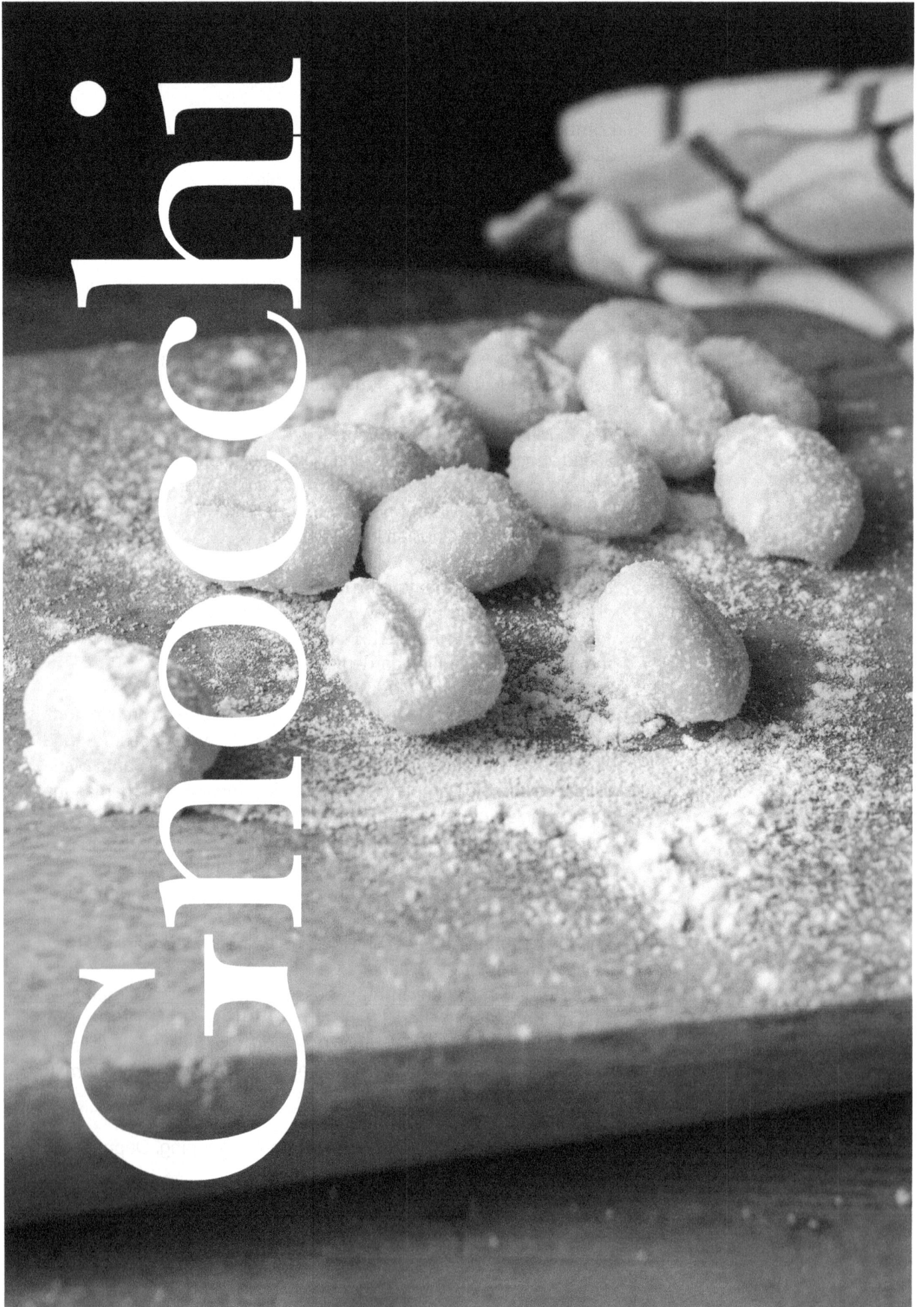

Gnocchi

Homemade pasta from Lombardia

Homemade pasta from Lombardia (Lombardy), a region in northern Italy, reflects the area's rich culinary diversity and its agricultural and dairy farming heritage. The pasta in Lombardy often incorporates local ingredients and flavors, resulting in unique dishes.

Pizzoccheri: Perhaps the most famous pasta from Lombardy, pizzoccheri are short, flat tagliatelle-like noodles made from buckwheat flour.

They are traditionally cooked with vegetables like Swiss chard or cabbage, and abundant amounts of local cheese (like Valtellina Casera), potatoes, and garlic, often finished with a generous amount of butter.

Casoncelli: Also known as "casunsei" in Lombard dialect, these are stuffed pasta similar to ravioli. The filling usually includes breadcrumbs, Parmigiano Reggiano, eggs, and ground meat (pork or beef), sometimes with a hint of garlic and parsley. They are typically served with melted butter, sage, and more grated Parmesan.

Ravioli o Tortelli di Zucca: These are pumpkin filled pasta common in Mantua, near Lombardy's southern border. The filling is a sweet-savory mix of pumpkin, amaretti cookies, and mostarda (candied fruit in a mustard flavored syrup), creating a unique flavor profile. They are often dressed simply with butter and sage.

Agnolini: Similar to tortellini, agnolini are small, stuffed pasta. They are usually filled with a mix of meat (like pork, beef, or chicken) and served in a rich broth, making them a staple in Lombardian comfort food, especially during holidays.

Gnocchi: While not unique to Lombardy, gnocchi is popular in the region. It can be made from potatoes or semolina and is often served with hearty sauces or simply with melted butter and sage.

The Pumpkin Gnocchi Became a Hit

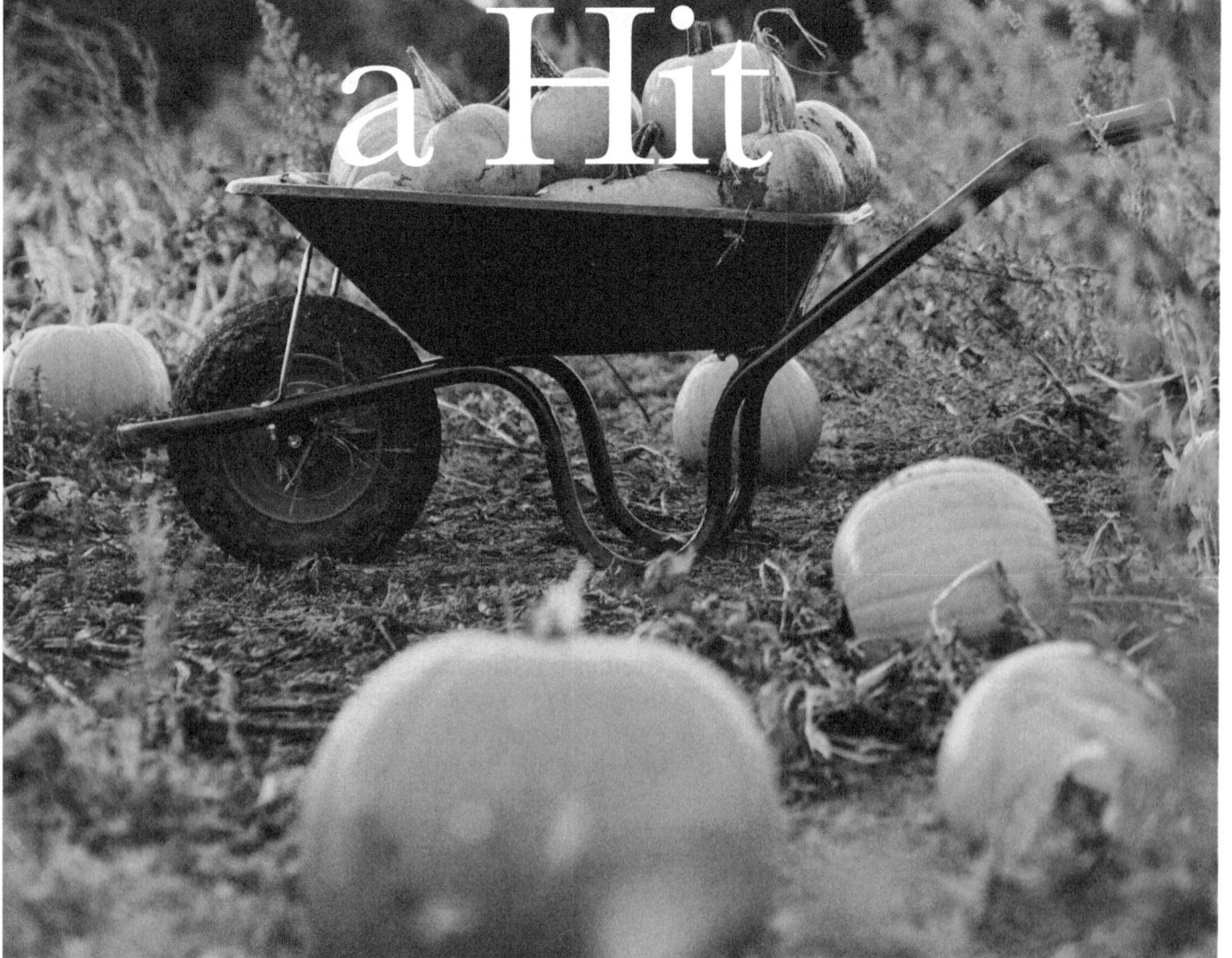

In Lombardy, the fertile plains and varied climate are ideal for growing a variety of crops, including pumpkins. Historically, pumpkins were an affordable and versatile ingredient for many local families, especially in lean times. The story goes that during a particularly poor harvest season, when wheat was scarce and expensive, inventive cooks in Lombardy turned to pumpkins, which were plentiful.

They discovered that the starchy nature of pumpkins made a great substitute for some of the flour in traditional potato gnocchi. By combining pumpkin puree with flour and sometimes potatoes, they created a new type of gnocchi that was not only economical but also had a unique, slightly sweet flavor and a vibrant orange color.

These pumpkin gnocchi became a hit, especially during autumn when pumpkins were in season. They were often served with butter and sage, Parmesan cheese, or even amaretti cookies crumbled on top to add a sweet contrast.

This adaptation of gnocchi reflects the creativity and resilience of the Lombard people in facing hardship. It also shows how regional cuisine can be influenced by local ingredients and the necessity to adapt to changing circumstances. To this day, Gnocchi di Zucca remains a beloved dish in Lombardy, cherished for its roots in local tradition and its delicious taste.

Pizzoccheri alla Valtellinese
Valtellinese-Style Pizzoccheri

Ingredients

Pizzoccheri (Buckwheat Pasta):
200 g buckwheat flour
100 g of regular flour
Water as needed

Sauce and Toppings:
2 medium potatoes, peeled and chopped
300 g of savoy cabbage or swiss chard chopped
2 cloves of garlic, minced
100 g of butter
150 g of grated Parmesan cheese
150 g of grated Valtellina Casera cheese (or Fontina)
Salt and pepper to taste

Instructions:

Make the Pasta:
Mix the buckwheat and regular flour. Gradually add water until you have a firm dough.
Roll out the dough thinly and cut into strips (about 7cm long and 1cm wide).

Cook the Vegetables and Pasta:
Boil the potatoes in salted water for about 10 minutes.
Add the cabbage or chard and cook for another 5 minutes.
Add the pizzoccheri pasta to the same pot and cook for about 5 minutes until the pasta is al dente.
In a separate pan, gently fry the minced garlic in butter until golden. Drain the pasta and vegetables, reserving a little of the cooking water.
Layer the pasta and vegetables with the cheeses in a serving dish, adding a little cooking water to keep it moist. Pour the garlic butter over the top. Serve hot, allowing the cheeses to melt and blend together.

Casoncelli alla Bergamasca
Bergamo-Style Casoncelli

Ingredients

For the Pasta Dough:
400 g of all-purpose flour
2 large eggs
Water as needed

For the Filling:
200 g of ground beef or pork
100g of mortadella or Italian sausage, finely chopped
50 g grated Parmesan cheese
50 g of bread crumbs
1 large Egg
2 Amaretti cookies, crushed
30 g of raisins
1 clove of garlic, minced
A pinch of nutmeg
Salt and pepper to taste

For the Sauce:
100 g of butter
A handful of sage leaves
Grated Parmesan cheese for serving

Instructions

Prepare the Pasta Dough:
Mix the flour and eggs together, adding a little water if necessary, to form a smooth and elastic dough.
Let it rest for 30 minutes, covered with a cloth.

Make the Filling:
In a bowl, mix the ground meat, mortadella, Parmesan, bread crumbs, egg, crushed amaretti, raisins, garlic, nutmeg, salt, and pepper until well combined.

Shape the Casoncelli:
Roll out the pasta dough thinly.
Place small amounts of filling on the dough, spaced evenly. Fold the dough over and cut into shapes using a pastry cutter. Boil the casoncelli in salted water for about 3-5 minutes or until they float to the surface.

Prepare the Sauce:
Melt the butter in a pan and add the sage leaves, cooking until the butter is slightly browned and fragrant. Drain the casoncelli and toss them in the sage butter.
Serve with a generous sprinkle of grated Parmesan cheese on top.

Ravioli di Zucca alla Mantovana
Mantuan Pumpkin Ravioli

Ingredients

For the Pasta Dough:
400 g of all-purpose flour
4 Large eggs
A pinch of salt

For the Filling:
600 g of pumpkin
(preferably a sweet variety like Butternut)
100 g of Mostarda di Cremona
(Italian candied fruit in mustard-flavored syrup),
finely chopped
100 g of Amaretti cookies, crushed
100 g of grated Parmesan cheese
Nutmeg to taste
Salt and pepper to taste

For the Sauce:
100 g of butter
A handful of sage leaves
Grated Parmesan cheese, for serving

Instructions

Prepare the Pasta Dough:
Combine the flour, eggs, and a pinch of salt. Knead to form a smooth, elastic dough. Let it rest for about 30 minutes, covered.
Cut the pumpkin into pieces, remove the seeds, and bake in the oven until tender (about 30-40 minutes at 180°C/355°F). Alternatively, you can boil it.
Once cooked, scoop out the flesh and mash it or pass it through a sieve to obtain a smooth puree.

Make the Filling:
Mix the pumpkin puree with the mostarda, crushed amaretti, Parmesan cheese, a pinch of nutmeg, and season with salt and pepper.
Roll out the pasta dough thinly. Place small spoonfuls of the pumpkin filling at intervals on the dough.
Fold the dough over the filling and cut into individual tortelli with a pastry cutter. Press the edges to seal.
Boil the tortelli in salted water until they float to the top, about 3-5 minutes. Melt the butter in a pan and add the sage leaves, cooking until the butter is slightly browned and fragrant. Drain the tortelli and gently toss them in the sage butter. Serve hot, sprinkled with additional grated Parmesan cheese.

Gnocchi al Gorgonzola
Gnocchi with Gorgonzola Cheese Sauce

Ingredients

For the Gnocchi:
1 kg of potatoes (preferably starchy, like Russets)
300 g of all-purpose flour
1 of egg
Salt to taste
For the Gorgonzola Sauce:
200 g of Gorgonzola cheese
(you can choose between sweet or spicy)
200 ml of heavy cream
50g of butter
A pinch of nutmeg
Salt and pepper to taste
Optional:
A handful of chopped walnuts or parsley for garnish

Instructions

Make the Gnocchi:
Boil the potatoes with their skins on until tender.
Peel while still warm and mash them until smooth.
Mix the mashed potatoes with flour, egg, and a pinch of salt to form a dough.
Roll the dough into long "snakes" and cut into small pieces to form gnocchi. Press each piece with a fork to give it the characteristic ridges.
Boil the gnocchi in salted water. They are done when they float to the surface.
Prepare the Gorgonzola Sauce:
In a pan, melt the butter over low heat. Add the Gorgonzola cheese and heavy cream, stirring until the cheese melts and the sauce becomes creamy. Season with a pinch of nutmeg, and salt and pepper to taste.
Drain the cooked gnocchi and add them to the sauce, gently tossing to coat. Serve immediately, optionally garnished with chopped walnuts or parsley for an added texture and flavor.

Piedmont

Known for its exquisite wines, sumptuous cuisine, and picturesque hills, offers an immersive experience into the heart of Italian elegance and charm.

A tour of Piemonte (Piedmont), a region in northwest Italy known for its rich history, stunning landscapes, and world renowned wines and cuisine, offers an unforgettable experience. Here's what a tour through Piedmont might include:

Day 1: Arrival in Turin

Start your journey in Turin, the capital of Piedmont, known for its refined architecture and cuisine.

Visit the Royal Palace of Turin, the Mole Antonelliana, and the National Cinema Museum. Stroll along the Po River and enjoy a traditional aperitivo in one of the city's elegant cafes.

Day 2: Turin's Museums and Markets

Dedicate another day to exploring Turin's rich cultural offerings, such as the Egyptian Museum or the Museum of Oriental Art.

Visit the bustling Porta Palazzo, Europe's largest open-air market, and sample local specialties.

In the evening, try Turin's renowned chocolate and coffee culture, perhaps visiting historic cafes like Caffè Al Bicerin.

Day 3: The Langhe Wine Region

Travel to the Langhe region, famous for its wines, such as Barolo and Barbaresco. Enjoy a day of wine tasting at various vineyards and learn about the wine-making process.

Explore charming towns like Alba, known for its white truffles, and Neive, one of Italy's most beautiful villages.

Day 4: The Monferrato Area

Visit the Monferrato area, another renowned wine region, part of the UNESCO World Heritage site together with Langhe and Roero. Explore towns like Asti, known for Asti Spumante (sparkling wine), and visit historical wineries. Enjoy the scenic landscapes of rolling hills and vineyards that characterize the region.

Day 5: The Royal Residences and Venaria Reale

Visit some of the Royal Residences of the House of Savoy, like the Palace of Venaria, a magnificent example of Baroque art and architecture. Stroll through the beautifully landscaped gardens and visit the art exhibitions housed within.

Day 6: The Mountains of Piedmont

Explore the Piedmontese Alps, offering breathtaking views and outdoor activities such as hiking or skiing (depending on the season). Visit towns like Sestriere, famous for winter sports, or the Val di Susa with its medieval abbeys and fortresses.

Day 7: Departure from Turin

Spend your last day in Turin visiting any missed sites, shopping for local products like wines, truffles, and chocolates. Depart from Turin's international airport or train station.

Tajarin

Homemade pasta from Piedmont

Homemade pasta from Piemonte (Piedmont), a region in northwest Italy, is known for its distinctive flavors and traditional preparation methods.

Here are some key types of pasta and dishes that are typical in Piemonte:

Tajarin (Tagliolini): Tajarin are thin, ribbon-like egg pasta, similar to tagliatelle but much finer. They are typically made with a high proportion of egg yolks, giving them a rich flavor and a golden color. Tajarin is often served with simple sauces, such as butter and sage or a meat ragù.

Agnolotti del Plin: Agnolotti is a type of ravioli typical of Piemonte, and 'del Plin' means 'pinched', referring to the technique used to seal the pasta. These small, pinched pasta parcels are typically filled with a mixture of roasted meats and vegetables. They are usually served with a simple sauce of butter and sage or sometimes meat broth.

Gnocchi di Patate: Potato gnocchi are common in Piemonte, often served with rich and hearty sauces, such as a Gorgonzola cheese sauce or a meat ragù.

Ravioli al Plin: Similar to Agnolotti del Plin, these are small ravioli filled with a meat mixture, pinched at the edges to seal. They are typically smaller than Agnolotti and can have different fillings, including cheese or vegetables.

Agnolotti del Plin al Sugo di Arrosto
Pinched Agnolotti with Roast Meat Sauce

Ingredients

For the Pasta Dough:
400 g of all-purpose flour
4 of large eggs
A pinch of salt

For the Filling:
200 g of roasted beef or pork, finely chopped
100 g of cooked spinach, finely chopped
50 g of grated Parmesan cheese
1 of small onion, finely chopped
1 of clove garlic, minced
1 of egg
Nutmeg, to taste
Salt and pepper, to taste

For the Sugo di Arrosto (Roast Meat Sauce):
300 g of roast beef or pork, chopped
1 of onion, finely chopped
1 of carrot, finely chopped
1 of celery stalk, finely chopped
1 of glass of red wine
Beef or chicken stock, as needed
Olive oil
Salt and pepper, to taste

Instructions

Prepare the Pasta Dough:
Combine flour, eggs, and a pinch of salt to form a dough. Knead until smooth and elastic. Let it rest for about 30 minutes.

Sauté onion and garlic until soft. Add the chopped roast beef or pork, and cook for a few minutes.

Remove from heat and let it cool. Then, mix in the spinach, Parmesan, egg, nutmeg, salt, and pepper.

Roll out the pasta dough thinly. Place small amounts of filling along the dough. Fold the dough over and pinch between each portion of filling to create the "plin" (pinch). Cut between each pinch to separate the agnolotti.

Prepare the Sugo di Arrosto:
In a pan, sauté onion, carrot, and celery with olive oil until softened. Add the chopped roast meat and brown it slightly. Pour in the red wine and let it reduce. Add enough stock to cover the meat and simmer until the sauce thickens. Boil the agnolotti in salted water until they float to the surface, about 3-5 minutes.

Drain the agnolotti and serve them with the warm sugo di arrosto. Garnish with grated Parmesan cheese and a sprinkle of fresh herbs if desired.

Agnolotti del Plin has been a family affair.

Agnolotti del Plin is a cherished pasta from Piedmont, Italy, with a unique history and making process.

The name "del Plin" means "a pinch," which refers to the pinching technique used to seal these small, stuffed pasta parcels. Here's an anecdote that illustrates the cultural significance and the communal aspect of making Agnolotti del Plin.

In the rural areas of Piedmont, preparing Agnolotti del Plin has traditionally been a family affair, often involving multiple generations. The story goes that during special occasions and big family gatherings, especially around the holidays, the entire family would come together to prepare Agnolotti del Plin. This wasn't just a culinary endeavor but a social event, a time for storytelling, sharing, and passing down family traditions.

The women of the family, who were usually responsible for cooking, would gather around a large table to roll out the pasta dough, prepare the filling (often a mix of roasted meats and herbs), and assemble the agnolotti. It was during this process that the "plin" technique – a simple pinch to seal the pasta – became a signature of the dish. This method not only efficiently sealed the agnolotti but also created a distinctive look that set it apart from other stuffed pastas.

Children were often taught how to "plin" from a young age, making this a rite of passage in many Piedmontese families. The act of pinching the pasta was more than just a culinary technique; it was a way to instill a sense of heritage and family identity in the younger members.

To this day, Agnolotti del Plin symbolizes the warmth of family gatherings and the transmission of culinary knowledge across generations in Piedmont. It's a testament to how food can be deeply intertwined with cultural identity, family, and tradition.

Tajerin al Tartufo Bianco d'Alba
Tagliolini with Alba White Truffle

Ingredients

For the Pasta Dough:
300 g of all-purpose flour
100 g of semolina flour
8 of egg yolks
2 of whole eggs
A pinch of salt
For the Sauce:
White truffles from Alba
(quantity as desired, usually a few grams per serving)
100g of unsalted butter
Salt, to taste
Freshly ground black pepper, to taste

Instructions

Make the Tajarin Pasta:
Combine both types of flour with a pinch of salt on a work surface. Make a well in the center and add the egg yolks and whole eggs.
Gradually incorporate the flour into the eggs until a dough forms. Knead until smooth.
Let the dough rest for about 30 minutes, then roll it out thinly (preferably with a pasta machine) and cut into thin strips (about 3mm wide).
Bring a large pot of salted water to a boil. Cook the tajarin until al dente (about 2-3 minutes).
Prepare the Truffle Sauce:
While the pasta is cooking, melt the butter in a large pan. Keep it warm but do not let it brown. Season with a little salt and black pepper.
Drain the pasta and add it to the pan with the melted butter. Toss gently to coat the pasta in the butter.
Serve the pasta in warm plates.
Finish with White Truffles:
Thinly shave the White Truffles from Alba over each plate of pasta. The heat from the pasta will release the truffle's aromatic oils.
Serve Immediately:
Enjoy this elegant dish immediately to savor the full aroma and flavor of the fresh truffles.
This dish is a celebration of simplicity and quality, letting the rare and aromatic White Truffles shine.

It's a true gourmet experience!

Gnocchi della Val Varaita
Gnocchi from Val Varaita

Ingredients
For the Gnocchi:
1 kg of potatoes
(preferably starchy ones like Russets)
300 g of all-purpose flour
1 of egg
Salt, to taste
For the Sauce:
200 g of fresh ricotta cheese
100 g of grated Parmesan cheese
A handful of fresh herbs (such as sage or thyme),
finely chopped
100 g of butter
Salt and pepper, to taste

Instructions
Make the Gnocchi:
Boil the potatoes with their skins on until tender.
Peel them while still warm and mash until smooth.
Combine the mashed potatoes with flour, egg, and
a pinch of salt, and knead to form a smooth dough.
Divide the dough into sections and roll each into long
"snakes" on a floured surface. Cut into small pieces
to form gnocchi. Press each piece against the tines
of a fork to create ridges.
Bring a large pot of salted water to a boil. Cook the
gnocchi in batches; they are done when they float
to the surface. Remove with a slotted spoon and set
aside. In a pan, melt the butter and add the chopped
herbs, cooking for a few minutes until fragrant.
Add the ricotta and Parmesan cheese to the pan,
stirring until the cheese melts and the sauce becomes
creamy. Season with salt and pepper.
Add the cooked gnocchi to the sauce, gently tossing
to coat them evenly. Serve hot, with an extra sprinkle
of Parmesan cheese if desired.

Trentino Alto Adige

A region renowned for its stunning natural landscapes and rich cultural heritage.

A tour of Trentino-Alto Adige, a region in northern Italy known for its stunning alpine scenery, unique cultural blend of Italian and Austrian influences, and outdoor activities, offers a memorable experience of nature, history, and culture.

Day 1: Arrival in Bolzano

Begin your journey in Bolzano, the capital city of South Tyrol, where Italian and German cultures blend. Visit the South Tyrol Museum of Archaeology to see Ötzi the Iceman, a well-preserved mummy from the Copper Age. Stroll through the city center, enjoying the medieval architecture and vibrant markets.

Day 2: The Dolomites and Val Gardena

Explore the Dolomites, a stunning mountain range and a UNESCO World Heritage site. Visit Val Gardena, a valley known for its woodcarving tradition and beautiful hiking trails. Enjoy outdoor activities like hiking in the summer or skiing in the winter.

Day 3: Merano and the Gardens of Trauttmansdorff Castle

Travel to Merano, a spa town with a mild climate and lush gardens. Visit the Gardens of Trauttmansdorff Castle, offering panoramic views and a variety of botanical landscapes. Explore Merano's thermal baths or walk along the Passer River promenade.

Day 4: Trento and the Trentino Side

Head to Trento, the capital of the Trentino region, with its rich Renaissance history. Visit the Castello del Buonconsiglio, Trento Cathedral, and the MUSE Science Museum. Sample local wines like Teroldego and Trentodoc sparkling wine.

Day 5: Lake Garda and Riva del Garda

Visit the northern shores of Lake Garda, Italy's largest lake, known for its Mediterranean climate and stunning scenery.

Explore Riva del Garda, with its charming old town, fortress, and lakeside promenade.

Enjoy water sports on the lake, such as sailing and windsurfing.

Day 6: The Wine Road and Caldaro Lake

Explore the South Tyrolean Wine Road, visiting vineyards and tasting local wines like Lagrein and Gewürztraminer.

Visit Caldaro Lake, the warmest lake in the Alps, and enjoy its beautiful surroundings. In the evening, try traditional Tyrolean dishes like knödel (dumplings) and speck (smoked ham).

Day 7: Departure from Bolzano or Trento

Spend your last day in either Bolzano or Trento, doing some last-minute shopping for local products like apple strudel, speck, and wine. Depart from Bolzano or Trento's train station or the nearest airport.

Knödel

Homemade pasta from Trentino Alto Adige

Homemade pasta from Trentino-Alto Adige, a region in northern Italy known for its unique blend of Italian and Austrian-German culinary traditions, showcases a variety of distinctive pasta types and dishes.

Canederli (Knödel): Although more of a dumpling than a pasta, canederli are a staple in Trentino-Alto Adige. Made from bread, milk, eggs, and speck (a local smoked ham), these dumplings are often served in broth or with a butter and sage sauce.

Spätzle: A type of soft egg noodle of German origin, spätzle in Trentino-Alto Adige is often made with spinach, giving it a green color. It's typically served with cheese, cream, or as a side dish to meaty stews.

Schlutzkrapfen: Similar to ravioli, these are half moon shaped stuffed pasta. The filling usually includes spinach and ricotta, and they are typically served with melted butter, sage, and parmesan.

Tagliatelle: While common throughout Italy, in Trentino Alto Adige, they might be served with game meat sauces, such as deer or rabbit, reflecting the region's alpine environment.

Casunziei: These are half-moon shaped pasta similar to ravioli, originating from the Dolomites area. They are typically filled with beetroot and ricotta and served with melted butter and poppy seeds.

Spätzle allo Speck
Spätzle with Speck

Ingredients

For the Spatzle:
400 g of all-purpose flour
4 of large eggs
120 ml of water (approximately)
1/2 teaspoon of salt
Nutmeg, to taste

For the Sauce and Toppings:
200 g of Speck (smoked, cured ham), cut into strips or cubes
1 of large onion, finely chopped
2 tablespoons of butter
Salt and pepper, to taste
Fresh parsley, chopped (for garnish)
Grated Parmesan cheese (optional)

Instructions

Make the Spatzle:
In a large bowl, mix together the flour, eggs, salt, and a pinch of nutmeg. Gradually add the water, mixing until the batter is smooth but still thick.
Let the batter rest for about 30 minutes.
Bring a large pot of salted water to a boil. Use a spatzle maker or a colander with large holes to press the batter into the boiling water.
Cook the spatzle until they float to the surface, then remove them with a slotted spoon and drain.

Prepare the Sauce:
In a large skillet, melt the butter over medium heat.
Add the chopped onion and cook until translucent.
Add the speck and cook until it starts to crisp up.
Season with salt and pepper.
Add the drained spatzle to the skillet with the speck and onion. Toss everything together and cook for a few more minutes until the spatzle are well coated and heated through. Serve the spatzle with speck hot, garnished with chopped parsley. Optionally, you can sprinkle grated Parmesan cheese on top.

Canederli allo Speck in Brodo
Speck Dumplings in Broth

Ingredients

For the Canederli (Dumplings):
250 g of stale bread, cut into cubes
100 g of Speck (smoked, cured ham), finely chopped
2 of large eggs
1/2 cup of milk
1 of small onion, finely chopped
2 tablespoons of butter
2 tablespoons of all-purpose flour
A handful of fresh parsley, chopped
Salt and pepper, to taste
A pinch of nutmeg

For the Brodo (Broth):
1.5 liters of chicken or beef broth
1 of carrot, chopped
1 of celery stalk, chopped
1 of onion, chopped
Salt and pepper, to taste

Instructions

Prepare the Canederli Mixture:
In a skillet, melt the butter and sauté the chopped onion until translucent. Add the speck and cook for a few minutes. Set aside to cool.
In a large bowl, soak the bread cubes in milk until soft. Add the cooled speck and onion mixture, eggs, flour, parsley, salt, pepper, and nutmeg to the bread. Mix well. If the mixture is too dry, add a bit more milk; if too wet, add a bit more flour.
Let the mixture rest for about 30 minutes.

Shape the Canederli:
With moistened hands, form the mixture into balls about the size of a golf ball.

Prepare the Broth:
In a large pot, bring the broth to a simmer with the carrot, celery, and onion. Season with salt and pepper.

Cook the Canederli:
Gently place the canederli in the simmering broth. Let them cook for about 15 minutes or until they float to the surface. Serve the canederli in bowls with the hot broth. Garnish with additional chopped parsley or chives, if desired.

Nothing was wasted, not even stale bread...

This hearty dumpling dish has an interesting anecdote that reflects the region's history and culinary ingenuity. The story dates back to a time when resources were scarce, and food conservation was crucial. In the Alpine households of Trentino-Alto Adige, nothing was wasted, not even stale bread. Housewives, known for their resourcefulness, sought ways to use up leftover bread. They began to mix small pieces of stale bread with milk, eggs, and some basic seasonings, such as onions and parsley, to create a simple yet filling meal. Over time, other ingredients like speck (a type of local smoked ham), cheese, or spinach were added to enhance the flavor.

Originally, Knödel was considered a poor man's food, but it soon became a beloved staple, appreciated for its comforting flavors and the ability to keep bellies full during the harsh Alpine winters. The dumplings were typically cooked in broth, giving them a tender, moist texture, and were often served with a salad or sauerkraut on the side.

This transformation of a humble bread-based dish into a culinary staple is a testament to the ingenuity of the people in this region. It also shows how historical circumstances and cultural influences can shape a region's cuisine, turning simple ingredients into something special that is passed down through generations. Today, Knödel is celebrated as a key part of Trentino Alto Adige's culinary heritage, enjoyed by locals and visitors alike.

Schlutzkrapfen alla Tirolese
Tyrolean-style Schlutzkrapfen

Ingredients

For the Pasta Dough:
200 g of rye flour
200 g of all-purpose flour
1 of egg
Water, as needed
A pinch of salt

For the Filling:
250 g of fresh spinach
1 of small onion, finely chopped
1 clove of garlic, minced
150 g of ricotta cheese
50 g of grated Parmesan cheese
Nutmeg, to taste
Salt and pepper, to taste

To Serve:
Melted butter
Grated Parmesan cheese
Fresh chives, chopped

Instructions

Make the Pasta Dough:
Combine the rye and all-purpose flours with a pinch of salt. Make a well in the center, add the egg, and gradually add enough water to form a smooth dough. Knead the dough until elastic, then cover and let it rest for about 30 minutes.

Prepare the Filling:
Blanch the spinach in boiling water, then drain and squeeze out excess water. Chop it finely.

In a pan, sauté the onion and garlic until soft. Add the spinach and cook for a few minutes.

Remove from heat and let it cool. Mix in the ricotta, Parmesan, nutmeg, salt, and pepper.

Assemble the Schlutzkrapfen:
Roll out the pasta dough thinly. Cut out circles using a cookie cutter or a glass.

Place a small amount of filling on one half of each circle. Fold the dough over to form a half-moon shape and press the edges to seal.

Bring a large pot of salted water to a boil. Cook the schlutzkrapfen in batches for about 3-4 minutes, or until they float to the surface. Drain the schlutzkrapfen and serve with melted butter, a sprinkle of Parmesan, and chopped chives.

Tagliatelle ai Finferli
Tagliatelle with Chanterelle Mushrooms

Ingredients

For the Homemade Tagliatelle:
400 g of all-purpose flour
4 of large eggs
A pinch of salt

For the Finferli Sauce:
400 g of chanterelle mushrooms (finferli),
cleaned and sliced
2 cloves of garlic, minced
4 tablespoons of olive oil
200 ml of heavy cream
A small bunch of fresh parsley,
finely chopped
Salt and pepper, to taste
Grated Parmesan cheese, for serving

Instructions

Make the Tagliatelle:
On a clean surface, make a mound with the flour and create a well in the center. Crack the eggs into the well and add a pinch of salt.

Gradually mix the flour into the eggs until a dough forms. Knead the dough for about 10 minutes until smooth and elastic. Cover the dough with a cloth and let it rest for 30 minutes.

Roll out the dough thinly, then cut it into long, narrow ribbons (tagliatelle). Let them dry slightly while you prepare the sauce.

Prepare the Chanterelle Sauce:
Heat the olive oil in a large skillet over medium heat. Add the minced garlic and sauté until fragrant but not browned. Add the chanterelle mushrooms and cook until they're tender and have released their moisture. Pour in the heavy cream and bring to a simmer.

Reduce the heat and let the sauce thicken slightly. Season with salt and pepper.

Stir in the chopped parsley.

Bring a large pot of salted water to a boil.

Cook the homemade tagliatelle until al dente, about 2-3 minutes. Drain the pasta, reserving a little pasta water. Toss the cooked tagliatelle with the chanterelle sauce, adding a bit of the reserved pasta water if needed to loosen the sauce. Serve hot, garnished with grated Parmesan cheese.

Veneto

A region famed for its romantic landscapes, rich history, and exceptional culinary traditions.

A tour of Veneto, a region in northeastern Italy known for its diverse landscapes ranging from the Adriatic Sea to the Dolomite mountains, as well as its rich history and artistic heritage, offers a varied and enriching experience.

Day 1: Arrival in Venice

Begin your journey in Venice, the capital of the Veneto region, famed for its canals, Gothic architecture, and artistic heritage. Explore the iconic St. Mark's Square, visit St. Mark's Basilica and the Doge's Palace. Enjoy a gondola ride through the canals and explore the winding streets of the city.

Day 2: More of Venice and its Islands

Dedicate another day to exploring Venice. Visit the Rialto Bridge and market, and the Accademia Gallery. Take a boat trip to the islands of Murano, known for glassmaking, and Burano, famous for its lace and brightly colored houses.

Day 3: Verona and Valpolicella

Travel to Verona, the city of Romeo and Juliet. Visit Juliet's House, the Roman Arena, and the historic city center. In the afternoon, explore the Valpolicella wine region, known for Amarone wine. Enjoy a wine tasting at a local vineyard.

Day 4: The Dolomites and Cortina d'Ampezzo

Head to the Dolomites, a stunning mountain range and UNESCO World Heritage site. Visit Cortina d'Ampezzo, a renowned ski resort and a hub for outdoor activities like hiking and mountain biking. Enjoy the breathtaking mountain views and explore the surrounding nature.

Day 5: Padua and the Euganean Hills

Visit Padua, known for the Scrovegni Chapel with frescoes by Giotto, and the historic University of Padua. In the afternoon, explore the Euganean Hills, an area of thermal baths and beautiful landscapes. Visit Arquà Petrarca, a medieval village where the poet Petrarch spent his last years.

Day 6: Vicenza and the Palladian Villas

Travel to Vicenza, a city famous for the architectural works of Andrea Palladio. Visit the Teatro Olimpico and Palladian Basilica. Explore the Palladian Villas of the Veneto in the countryside, which are part of the UNESCO World Heritage.

Day 7: Departure from Venice

Spend your last day in Venice, perhaps visiting the Peggy Guggenheim Collection or enjoying a leisurely walk along the Grand Canal. Depart from Venice's Marco Polo Airport or Santa Lucia train station.

Bigoli

Homemade pasta from Veneto

In the Veneto region of Italy, known for its rich culinary heritage, several types of homemade pasta are popular.

Bigoli: This is a thick, long pasta similar to spaghetti but larger in diameter. Traditionally, it's made with whole wheat flour and often served with rich sauces.

Pasta e Fagioli: While this is more of a dish than a type of pasta, it often includes homemade pasta in a bean-based soup. It's a classic Italian comfort food.

Gnocchi: Veneto has its own version of gnocchi, often made with potatoes. These soft dough dumplings are a staple in Italian cuisine and are served with various sauces.

Lasagne: While lasagna is common throughout Italy, the Veneto region has its unique spin on this classic, often incorporating spinach into the pasta dough for a green color.

Fettuccine: Similar to tagliatelle, fettuccine is a type of pasta popular in Veneto, served with a variety of sauces.

Bigoli in Salsa alla Veneziana
Venetian-Style Bigoli in Sauce

Ingredients

For Homemade Bigoli Pasta:
400 gr. of all-purpose flour
4 large eggs
1 tablespoon olive oil
Salt, to taste
Semolina flour for dusting
For Salsa di Acciughe (Anchovy Sauce):
12 anchovy fillets (canned or fresh)
1 large onion, finely chopped
2 cloves of garlic, minced
60 ml (1/4 cup) extra virgin olive oil
Salt (to taste)
Freshly ground black pepper (to taste)
Optional: A pinch of red pepper flakes for heat
Fresh parsley, chopped (for garnish)

Instructions

Making the Bigoli Pasta:
Combine the all-purpose flour and a pinch of salt in a large bowl. Make a well in the center. Crack the eggs into the well and add the olive oil.
Gradually incorporate the flour into the eggs and oil, mixing to form a dough. Knead the dough on a lightly floured surface until it's smooth and elastic, about 10 minutes. If the dough is too sticky, add a little more flour.
Shape the Bigoli:
If you have a bigoli press (bigolaro), use it to shape the pasta. Otherwise, roll the dough into thin logs and use a pasta machine or a knife to cut them into long, thick spaghetti-like strands. Dust the shaped bigoli with semolina flour to prevent sticking.
Bring a large pot of salted water to a boil. Cook the bigoli until al dente, usually about 2-3 minutes for fresh pasta. Then drain, reserving some pasta water.
Making the Salsa di Acciughe:
Heat the olive oil in a large skillet over medium heat. Add the chopped onion and garlic, sautéing until they are soft and translucent. Reduce the heat to low and add the anchovy fillets. Break them down with a wooden spoon, allowing them to melt into the oil and create a rich sauce. Add red pepper flakes if desired. Toss the cooked bigoli with the anchovy sauce. Add a bit of the reserved pasta water if needed to adjust the consistency of the sauce. Season with salt and black pepper to taste. Garnish with chopped parsley.

Pasta e Fagioli di Lamon
Pasta and Bean Soup from Lamon

Ingredients

For the Homemade Pasta:
200 grams (about 2 cups) of all-purpose flour
2 large eggs
Salt, to taste
Semolina flour for dusting

For the Soup:
250 gr. (about 1 cup) Lamon beans
(or Borlotti beans), soaked overnight
1 onion, finely chopped
1 carrot, diced
1 stalk of celery, diced
2-3 cloves of garlic, minced
400 grams (about 14 ounces) canned tomatoes
or fresh ripe tomatoes, chopped
1 liter (about 4 cups) vegetable or chicken broth
Olive oil
Salt and pepper to taste
Fresh herbs (like rosemary or thyme), finely chopped
Parmesan cheese, grated (for serving)
Optional: Pancetta or bacon, diced

Instructions

Making the Pasta:
On a clean surface or in a large bowl, mix the flour with a pinch of salt. Create a well in the center and add the eggs. Gradually incorporate the flour into the eggs, mixing to form a dough. Knead the dough until smooth and elastic, about 10 minutes. Use additional flour if the dough is too sticky.

Roll the dough out on a floured surface to your desired thickness. Then, cut it into small shapes suitable for soup, like small squares or short strips.

Dust the pasta with semolina flour and set aside.

Making the Soup:
Drain the soaked beans. In a large pot, cover them with fresh water, bring to a boil, then simmer until tender (about 1-2 hours).

In another pot, heat olive oil. Add pancetta or bacon if using, and cook until slightly crispy. Add onion, carrot, celery, and garlic, cooking until they are soft.

Add cooked beans and tomatoes to the pot with vegetables. Pour in the broth and bring to a boil. Simmer for about 30 minutes. Add the homemade pasta to the soup and cook until the pasta is al dente, about 3-5 minutes, depending on the thickness. Season with salt, pepper, and fresh herbs.

Serve with grated Parmesan cheese.

Lasagne Radicchio e Monte Veronese
Lasagna with Radicchio and Typical Veronese Cheese

Ingredients

For the Homemade Lasagna Sheets:
300 gr. (about 2 cups) of all-purpose flour
3 large eggs
A pinch of salt
Water, as needed

For the Lasagna Filling:
1 large head of radicchio, thinly sliced
250 grams (about 8.8 ounces) of Monte Veronese cheese, grated or thinly sliced
300 ml (about 1 ¼ cups) of béchamel sauce (you can make this with butter, flour, milk, and a pinch of nutmeg)
Olive oil
Salt and pepper to taste
Grated Parmesan cheese for topping
Optional: white wine for cooking radicchio

Instructions

Making the Lasagna Sheets:
Mix the flour and salt on a clean surface or in a bowl. Create a well in the center and crack the eggs into it. Gradually incorporate the flour into the eggs to form a dough. Knead the dough until smooth and elastic, about 10 minutes. Add a little water if the dough is too dry. Roll the dough into thin sheets using a pasta machine or a rolling pin. The sheets should be thin enough to become slightly translucent.
Cut the sheets into lasagna-sized pieces and set aside on a semolina-dusted surface.

Preparing the Filling:
Heat olive oil in a pan over medium heat.
Add the sliced radicchio, seasoning with salt and pepper. You can add a splash of white wine for extra flavor. Cook until the radicchio is wilted and slightly caramelized.
Preheat your oven to 180°C (350°F). In a baking dish, start with a layer of lasagna sheets. Add a layer of cooked radicchio, then a layer of Monte Veronese cheese, and top with a layer of béchamel sauce.
Repeat the layers (pasta, radicchio, cheese, béchamel) until all ingredients are used, finishing with a layer of béchamel and cheese.
Bake in the preheated oven for about 30-40 minutes, or until the top is golden and bubbly.
Let the lasagna rest for a few minutes after taking it out of the oven. Serve warm, optionally topped with grated Parmesan cheese.

Friuli Venezia Giulia

The region is famous
for its wines.
Its cuisine is a blend
of Italian, Austrian,
and Slavic influences,
offering a unique
gastronomic experience.

A tour of Friuli Venezia Giulia, a region in northeastern Italy, offers a unique blend of diverse cultures, languages, and landscapes. This area, where Slavic, Germanic, and Latin cultures converge, boasts stunning alpine scenery, beautiful coastlines, historic cities, and a rich culinary tradition.

Day 1: Arrival in Trieste

Start in Trieste, the capital of the region, known for its Habsburg legacy and vibrant coffee culture.

Explore Piazza Unità d'Italia, one of Europe's largest sea-facing squares, and visit the historic Caffè degli Specchi.

Walk along the Molo Audace pier for views of the Gulf of Trieste.

Day 2: The Miramare Castle and the Carso

Visit the Miramare Castle, set on a cliff overlooking the sea, with its beautiful park.

Explore the Carso plateau, known for its unique terrain and caves, including the Grotta Gigante.

Enjoy a wine tasting session, sampling the region's distinctive wines like Terrano and Vitovska.

Day 3: Udine and Cividale del Friuli

Travel to Udine, a city with Venetian influences, and explore its Renaissance piazzas and the castle.

Visit Cividale del Friuli, a UNESCO World Heritage site, known for its Devil's Bridge and Lombard Temple.

Enjoy Friulian cuisine, perhaps trying frico (cheese and potato pancake) and local prosciutto.

Day 4: The Alps and Alpine Lakes

Head to the Carnia and the Julian Alps, experiencing the region's stunning mountain scenery.

Visit the Fusine Lakes, two beautiful alpine lakes, offering picturesque walking trails. Explore typical mountain villages and enjoy local specialties like polenta and Montasio cheese.

Day 5: The Coastal Town of Grado and Aquileia

Visit Grado, an island town known for its beaches and historic center. Explore the nearby ancient Roman city of Aquileia, a UNESCO World Heritage site, with its impressive basilica and mosaics. Enjoy fresh seafood in Grado, sampling dishes like "boreto a la graisana" (fish stew).

Day 6: The Slovenian Border and Gorizia

Explore the area near the Slovenian border, emphasizing the region's multicultural heritage. Visit Gorizia, a town that straddles Italy and Slovenia, with its medieval castle and historical museum. Taste the fusion of Italian and Slavic flavors in the local cuisine.

Day 7: Departure from Trieste

Spend your last day in Trieste, perhaps visiting the Revoltella Museum or taking a leisurely walk in the Roseto di San Giovanni. Depart from Trieste's international airport or train station.

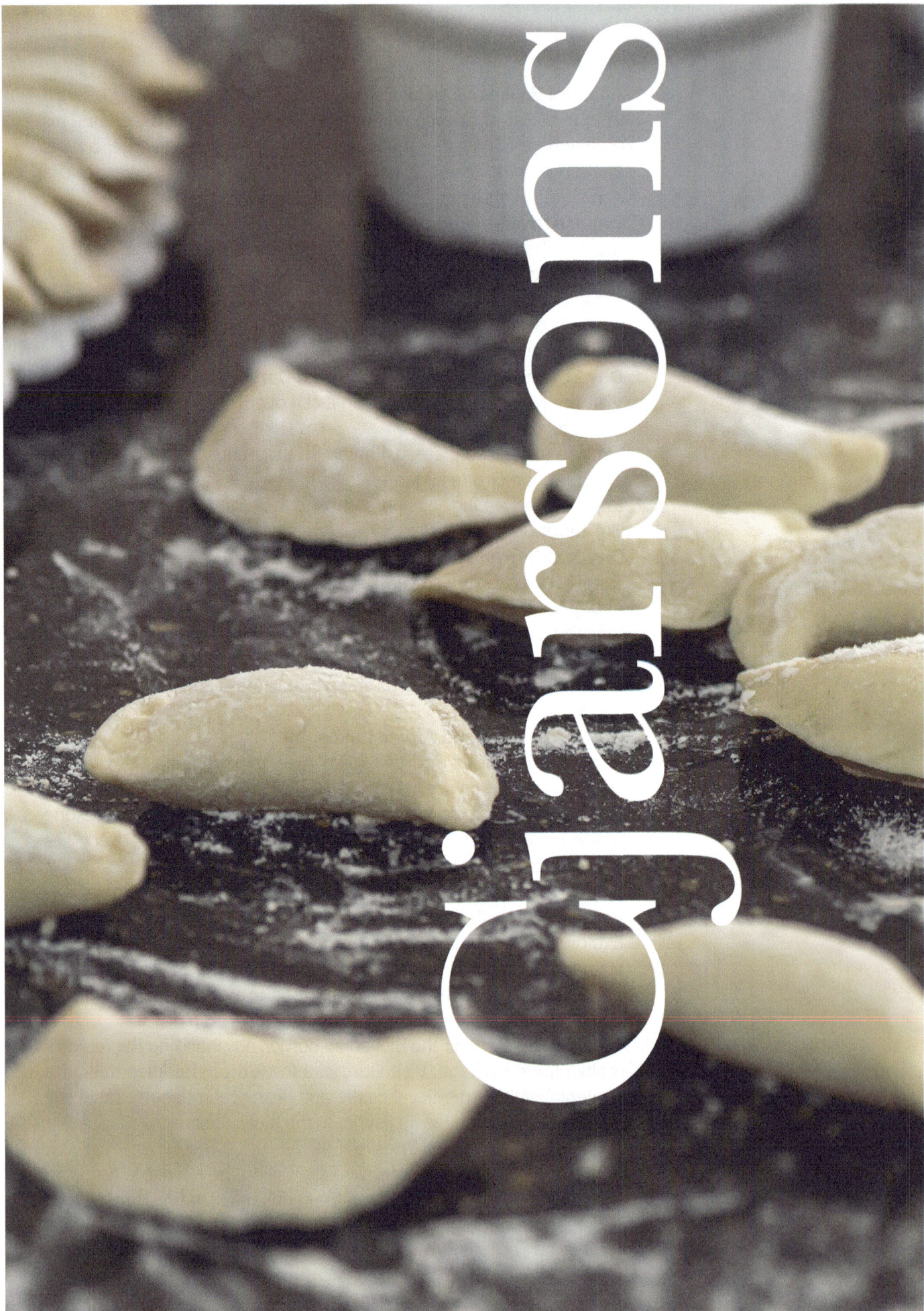

Cjarsons

Homemade pasta from Friuli Venezia Giulia

Homemade pasta from Friuli Venezia Giulia, a region in northeastern Italy, reflects the area's rich cultural mosaic and diverse culinary influences.

The pasta here is distinct, blending Italian, Slavic, and Austro-Hungarian traditions.

Cjarsons: A unique type of stuffed pasta that epitomizes the blend of cultures in Friuli Venezia Giulia. Cjarsons are similar to ravioli but with a more eclectic mix of sweet and savory fillings, which can include herbs, ricotta, potatoes, cocoa, and raisins, among others. They are typically served with melted butter, smoked ricotta, or poppy seeds.

Gnocchi: While gnocchi is popular throughout Italy, Friuli Venezia Giulia has its own variations. Gnocchi can be made from potatoes or bread and are often flavored with plums or prunes, reflecting the region's Slavic influences.

Blecs: A type of pasta similar to tagliatelle but irregularly shaped, often made with a mix of wheat and buckwheat flours. They are typically served with game meat sauces, mushrooms, or cheese.

Fusi: A type of pasta similar to thick spaghetti, often served with hearty stews or game meat sauces.

Cjarsons della Carnia
Cjarsons Carnia-Style

Ingredients

For the Dough:
400 gr. (about 3 1/3 cups) of all-purpose flour
200 ml (about 3/4 cup) of water
A pinch of salt

For the Filling:
250g (about 1 cup) of ricotta cheese
50g (about 1/3 cup) of raisins
50g (about 1/3 cup) of grated dark chocolate
30g (about 1/4 cup) of crushed amaretti biscuits
30g (about 1/4 cup) of sugar
1 small potato, boiled and mashed
A handful of chopped fresh parsley
A pinch of cinnamon
Salt to taste

For Serving:
Melted butter
Grated smoked ricotta or Parmesan cheese
Chopped fresh herbs (optional)

Instructions

Prepare the Dough:
Mix the flour with a pinch of salt in a bowl.
Gradually add water, mixing until a firm dough forms.
Knead the dough on a floured surface until smooth.
Let it rest, covered, for about 30 minutes.

Make the Filling:
In a bowl, mix together the ricotta, raisins, grated chocolate, crushed amaretti biscuits, sugar, mashed potato, chopped parsley, a pinch of cinnamon, and salt.

Assemble the Cjarsons:
Roll out the dough thinly on a floured surface.
Cut out circles using a cookie cutter or a glass.
Place a small spoonful of filling in the center of each circle. Fold the dough over the filling and seal the edges, creating a half-moon shape. Ensure the edges are tightly sealed to prevent the filling from leaking out during cooking.
Bring a large pot of salted water to a boil. Gently place the cjarsons in the boiling water and cook for about 3-5 minutes, or until they float to the surface.
Drain the cjarsons and serve hot, topped with melted butter, grated smoked ricotta or Parmesan cheese, and, if desired, some chopped fresh herbs.

Carnia, a region
with a history
of poverty
and scarcity,
but also immense
culinary creativity

One intriguing anecdote about Cjarsons encapsulates the diversity and richness of the culinary traditions in Carnia, a region with a history of poverty and scarcity, but also immense culinary creativity. Cjarsons combine sweet and savory flavors, reflecting the various cultural influences that have touched this region, from Austrian to Slavic and Venetian.

Traditionally, Cjarsons were made only on special occasions, particularly religious festivals and celebrations like Christmas. Women from different families in the villages would gather together to prepare Cjarsons, each bringing her own ingredients to contribute. This communal cooking turned into a festive event, where recipes and techniques were shared and passed down through generations.

The ingredients for the filling varied significantly from one valley to another, and even from one family to another, reflecting the diversity of the local produce and individual family traditions. Typically, the filling might include a mixture of sweet and savory elements like herbs, ricotta, potatoes, dried fruit, and cocoa, creating a unique flavor profile that is distinctly characteristic of Cjarsons.

One of the most interesting aspects of Cjarsons is this variety - there's no single "authentic" recipe, but rather a tapestry of recipes that together tell the story of the region's history, culture, and the resourcefulness of its people. This diversity in recipes not only underscores the adaptability of the people of Carnia but also illustrates how food can be a powerful expression of cultural identity.

Blecs al Sugo di Pomodoro
Blecs with Tomato Sauce

Ingredients

For the Dough:
300 gr. (about 2 cups) of all-purpose flour
2 large eggs
A pinch of salt
Water, as needed

For the Sugo di Pomodoro (Tomato Sauce):
1 can (about 400 gr.) of whole peeled tomatoes, crushed
2 cloves of garlic, minced
1 small onion, finely chopped
2 tablespoons of olive oil
A handful of fresh basil leaves
Salt and pepper to taste
Optional: red pepper flakes for heat

Instructions

Prepare the Dough:
On a clean surface or in a large bowl, mix the flour and salt. Make a well in the center and add the eggs. Gradually incorporate the flour into the eggs to form a dough. If the dough is too dry, add a little water.
Knead the dough until smooth and elastic, about 10 minutes.
Roll the dough out on a floured surface to a thickness of about 2-3 mm. Cut the dough into irregular squares or rectangles (blecs), approximately 5 cm in size.
Bring a large pot of salted water to a boil.
Cook the blecs in batches until they float to the surface, about 2-3 minutes. Remove them with a slotted spoon and set aside.

Making the Sugo di Pomodoro:
In a saucepan, heat the olive oil over medium heat. Add the minced garlic and chopped onion, and sauté until the onion is translucent. Add the crushed tomatoes to the saucepan. Season with salt, pepper, and red pepper flakes (if using). Bring the sauce to a simmer and cook for about 15-20 minutes, allowing the flavors to meld. Add the fresh basil leaves in the last few minutes of cooking. Add the cooked blecs to the tomato sauce, tossing gently to coat the pasta.
Serve hot, garnished with additional fresh basil or grated Parmesan cheese if desired.

Gnocchi de Susini alla Triestina
Trieste-Style Plum Gnocchi

Ingredients

For the Gnocchi:
1 kg (about 2.2 pounds) potatoes, preferably starchy variety
300 gr. (about 2 1/2 cups) all-purpose flour, plus extra for dusting
1 egg
A pinch of salt

For the Filling:
12-15 small plums (the number may vary based on size)
Sugar (to taste)
Cinnamon (optional)

For the Sauce:
100 gr. (about 1/2 cup) unsalted butter
Breadcrumbs, as needed
Sugar, for sprinkling
Optional: cinnamon or grated lemon zest for extra flavor

Instructions

Boil the potatoes in their skins until tender.
Once cooked, peel them while still hot and mash them until smooth. Allow the mashed potatoes to cool slightly.

Make the Gnocchi Dough:
To the mashed potatoes, add the flour, egg, and a pinch of salt. Knead the mixture to form a smooth dough. Be careful not to overwork it, as this can make the gnocchi tough.

Prepare the Plums:
Wash the plums, pat them dry, and slit them open to remove the pits. Stuff each plum with a little sugar (and a pinch of cinnamon if you like).

Divide the dough into small portions. Flatten each piece and place a stuffed plum in the center.
Encase each plum with the dough, forming a round gnocchi shape. Make sure the plums are completely covered. Bring a large pot of salted water to a boil.
Cook the gnocchi in batches. They are done when they float to the surface, about 3-4 minutes.
Remove with a slotted spoon and drain.

Prepare the Sauce:
In a pan, melt the butter. Add breadcrumbs to the melted butter and cook until they are golden brown.
Place the cooked gnocchi on a serving dish. Pour the buttery breadcrumb mixture over the gnocchi.
Sprinkle with sugar (and optionally cinnamon or lemon zest) before serving.

Emilia Romagna

Where every bite tells a story. Culinary traditions, medieval cities, Renaissance art.

A tour of Emilia-Romagna, a region in northern Italy known for its rich culinary traditions, medieval cities, and Renaissance art, offers a blend of cultural and gastronomic experiences.

Day 1: Arrival in Bologna

Start your journey in Bologna, the capital of Emilia-Romagna. Explore the historic city center, with its medieval towers, the Piazza Maggiore, and the Basilica di San Petronio. Enjoy a traditional Bolognese dinner, perhaps trying the famous tagliatelle al ragù.

Day 2: The Culinary Heart of Italy

Participate in a cooking class to learn how to make classic Emilia Romagnan dishes, such as tortellini and Bolognese sauce.

In the afternoon, visit a local producer of Parmigiano-Reggiano cheese and learn about its production process. Enjoy an evening of wine tasting, featuring regional wines like Lambrusco.

Day 3: Modena's Charm

Travel to Modena, known for its balsamic vinegar and the Enzo Ferrari Museum. Visit traditional balsamic vinegar producers to understand the aging process and enjoy a tasting session. Explore Modena's historical sites, including the Modena Cathedral and Piazza Grande, both UNESCO World Heritage Sites.

Day 4: Parma's Delights

Head to Parma, famous for Parma ham (Prosciutto di Parma) and Parmesan cheese. Tour a Prosciutto di Parma factory and enjoy a tasting. Spend the afternoon visiting the Parma Cathedral and the Teatro Farnese.

Day 5: The Po Delta and Ferrara

Explore the Po Delta, a unique wetland ecosystem and a UNESCO World Heritage Site. Continue to Ferrara, a Renaissance city known for its castle, cathedral, and medieval streets. Try some local Ferrara specialties, like cappellacci di zucca (pumpkin-filled pasta).

Day 6: Ravenna's Byzantine Mosaics

Visit Ravenna, famous for its stunning Byzantine mosaics.

Explore the Basilica of San Vitale, the Mausoleum of Galla Placidia, and other mosaic-adorned monuments.

In the afternoon, relax on the Adriatic coast, enjoying the beaches near Ravenna.

Day 7: Departure

Return to Bologna for any last-minute sightseeing or shopping.

Enjoy a final meal in Emilia-Romagna, perhaps trying some lesser known regional dishes.

Depart from Bologna's international airport or train station.

Tortellini

Homemade pasta from Emilia Romagna

Homemade pasta from Emilia-Romagna, a region in Northern Italy renowned for its rich culinary traditions, is celebrated for its variety, quality, and the skill involved in its preparation. Here are some key aspects of Emilia Romagnan homemade pasta:

Egg Pasta: Unlike some southern regions of Italy where pasta is often made with just water and flour, Emilia-Romagna is famous for its egg pasta. The dough typically consists of soft wheat flour and a high proportion of eggs, giving it a distinctive yellow color and rich flavor.

Tagliatelle: One of the most iconic pasta types from this region is tagliatelle, a long, flat ribbon-like pasta. It's traditionally served with a rich meat sauce, commonly known as Bolognese sauce.

Tortellini and Tortelloni: Emilia-Romagna is the birthplace of tortellini, small stuffed pasta shapes traditionally filled with a mixture of meats, cheese, and sometimes nutmeg. Tortelloni, their larger counterparts, are typically filled with ricotta and spinach or other vegetables.

Lasagne: Although lasagne is now made all over Italy and beyond, it originated in this region. Classic Emilia-Romagnan lasagne is made with green pasta (colored with spinach), layered with ragù, béchamel sauce, and Parmigiano-Reggiano cheese.

Cappelletti: Similar to tortellini but with a slightly different shape, cappelletti are typically served in a capon or chicken broth. They are usually filled with a mix of cheeses, meats, and sometimes lemon zest.

Pisarei: A traditional type of pasta originating from the town of Piacenza. They are small, gnocchi-like dumplings, typically made from a mixture of flour and breadcrumbs, sometimes with the addition of water or milk to form a dough.

Tagliatelle al Ragù alla Bolognese
Tagliatelle with Bolognese Sauce

Ingredients

For the Homemade Tagliatelle:
400 gr. (about 3 cups) of all-purpose flour, plus extra for dusting
4 large eggs
A pinch of salt
For the Ragù alla Bolognese:
300 gr. (about 2/3 lb) ground beef
150 gr. (about 1/3 lb) ground pork (optional, can use all beef)
1 medium carrot, finely chopped
1 celery stalk, finely chopped
1 medium onion, finely chopped
2 cloves garlic, minced
800 gr. (about 28 ounces) canned whole tomatoes, crushed
1 cup dry red wine
2 tablespoons olive oil
1 cup beef or chicken broth
2 tablespoons tomato paste
Salt and pepper to taste
A pinch of nutmeg

Instructions

Making the Tagliatelle:
Place the flour on a clean surface, forming a mound. Make a well in the center and add the eggs and a pinch of salt. Gradually mix the flour into the eggs until a dough forms.
Knead the dough until smooth and elastic, about 10 minutes. If it's sticky, add a bit more flour.
Roll and Cut the Pasta:
Let the dough rest, covered, for 30 minutes. Roll out the dough into thin sheets using a pasta machine or a rolling pin. Cut the sheets into long, narrow ribbons (tagliatelle).
Making the Ragù alla Bolognese:
In a large pot, heat the olive oil over medium heat. Add the carrot, celery, onion, and garlic, cooking until softened. Increase the heat and add the ground meats, cooking until browned. Pour in the wine, letting it simmer until reduced. Stir in the crushed tomatoes, tomato paste, broth, nutmeg. Bring to a simmer, then reduce the heat to low. Cover and let it cook for at least 2 hours, stirring occasionally. Add more broth if the sauce becomes too thick. Bring a large pot of salted water to a boil. Toss the cooked tagliatelle with the ragù. Serve with grated Parmesan cheese and fresh basil if desired.

Tortellini alla Crema di Parmigiano
Tortellini with Parmesan Cream Sauce

Ingredients

For the Homemade Tortellini:
400 gr. (about 3 1/3 cups) all-purpose flour
4 large eggs
Water, as needed
Salt
For the Meat Filling:
200 grams (about 7 ounces)
mixed ground meat (pork, beef, and/or veal)
50 grams (about 1.7 ounces) prosciutto,
finely chopped
50 grams (about 1.7 ounces) mortadella,
finely chopped
50 grams (about 1.7 ounces) grated
Parmigiano Reggiano cheese
1 egg
Nutmeg, salt, and pepper to taste
For the Parmesan Cream Sauce:
300 ml of heavy cream
100 gr. of freshly grated Parmigiano Reggiano cheese
Salt and freshly ground black pepper to taste
A pinch of nutmeg (optional)

Instructions

Making the Tortellini: On a clean surface, make a mound out of the flour and create a well in the center. Crack the eggs into the well and add a pinch of salt. Gradually mix the flour into the eggs until a dough forms. Add a little water if needed. Knead the dough until it becomes smooth and elastic, about 10 minutes.
Let it rest covered for 30 minutes.
Make the Meat Filling: In a bowl, combine the ground meat, prosciutto, mortadella, Parmigiano Reggiano, egg, nutmeg, salt, and pepper. Mix well. Roll out the dough into thin sheets. Cut the sheets into 2-inch squares. Place a small amount of meat filling in the center of each square. Fold the dough into a triangle, then wrap the longer sides around your finger and press to seal, forming the classic tortellini shape. Bring a pot of salted water to a boil. Cook the tortellini in batches until they float to the top, about 3-5 minutes. Drain and set aside.
Making the Crema di Parmigiano: In a saucepan, heat the cream over medium-low heat. Gradually add the grated Parmigiano Reggiano, stirring continuously until the cheese is fully melted and the sauce is smooth. Season with salt, pepper, and a pinch of nutmeg. Add the cooked tortellini to the sauce and gently toss to coat. Serve the tortellini di carne alla crema di parmigiano hot, garnished with additional grated cheese or fresh herbs if desired.

...and love created the Tortellino

Tortellini, the famed stuffed pasta from Emilia Romagna, particularly from the city of Bologna, has an anecdote that is as rich and delightful as the dish itself. The legend behind the shape of tortellini is a charming tale that intertwines culinary art with whimsy and allure.

The story goes that Venus, the goddess of love, stayed at a tavern in the Emilia region. The innkeeper, struck by her beauty, couldn't resist the temptation to sneak a peek at her through the keyhole of her room. All he could see, however, was her navel. Captivated by its beauty, he rushed to his kitchen and created a pasta in its image, giving birth to the tortellini.

This tale, while likely apocryphal, captures the essence of Italian passion for beauty, art, and food.

It also demonstrates the whimsical nature of culinary inspiration and how it can come from the most unexpected places. The story has become such a beloved part of regional folklore that the Chamber of Commerce of Bologna keeps a gold replica of a tortellino in a velvet case.

Beyond the myth, tortellini is a serious business in Emilia-Romagna. Traditionally, they are filled with a mixture of pork, prosciutto, mortadella, and Parmigiano Reggiano cheese, then served in a rich broth.

Making tortellini by hand is a skill passed down through generations, often among women of the family, known as "sfogline." This tradition is a treasured part of family life and local culture, symbolizing the region's dedication to culinary excellence and the importance of preserving culinary heritage.

Lasagna alla Bolgnese
Bolognese Lasagna

Ingredients

For the Lasagna Sheets:
300 gr. (about 2 cups) all-purpose flour
3 large eggs
A pinch of salt

For the Bolognese Sauce:
500 gr. (about 1 pound) ground beef
1 small onion, finely chopped
1 carrot, finely chopped
1 celery stalk, finely chopped
2 cloves of garlic, minced
800 grams (about 28 ounces) canned crushed tomatoes
1 cup red wine
2 tablespoons olive oil
Salt and pepper to taste
A pinch of nutmeg
Fresh basil or bay leaves

For the Béchamel Sauce:
500 ml (about 2 cups) milk
50 grams (about 4 tablespoons) butter
40 grams (about 1/3 cup) all-purpose flour
Nutmeg, salt, and pepper to taste
100 gr. (about 1 cup) grated Parmigiano Reggiano cheese

Instructions

Making the Lasagna Sheets:
Mix the flour and salt, then make a well in the center. Add the eggs and gradually incorporate into the flour to form a dough. Knead until smooth. Let it rest for 30 minutes. Roll the dough into thin sheets using a pasta machine or rolling pin. Cut into lasagna sheet sizes and set aside on a floured surface.

Making the Bolognese Sauce: In a large pot, heat olive oil. Sauté onion, carrot, celery, and garlic until soft. Add the ground beef, cooking until browned. Pour in wine and let it reduce (if using).
Stir in the crushed tomatoes, nutmeg, and herbs. Season with salt and pepper. Simmer for about 1-2 hours on low heat.

Making the Béchamel Sauce: Melt butter in a saucepan, stir in flour to form a roux. Gradually whisk in milk to avoid lumps. Cook until it thickens. Season with nutmeg, salt, and pepper.

Assembling the Lasagna: Preheat your oven to 180°C (350°F). Lightly grease a baking dish. Start with a layer of béchamel on the bottom. Add a layer of lasagna sheets, followed by Bolognese sauce, béchamel, and a sprinkle of Parmigiano. Repeat layers, finishing with béchamel and Parmigiano on top. Cover with foil and bake for about 30 minutes. Uncover and bake for another 15 minutes until the top is golden. Let the lasagna rest for 10-15 minutes before serving.

Pisarei e Fasò
Pisarei and Beans

Ingredients

For the Pisarei:

200 gr. (about 1 2/3 cups) bread crumbs

200 gr. (about 1 2/3 cups) all-purpose flour

About 100 ml (a little less than 1/2 cup) water

A pinch of salt

For the Fasò (Bean Sauce):

400 grams (about 14 ounces) canned Borlotti beans, drained and rinsed

1 onion, finely chopped

1 carrot, finely chopped

1 celery stalk, finely chopped

1 clove garlic, minced

400 grams (about 14 ounces) canned peeled tomatoes, crushed

100 grams (about 3.5 ounces) pancetta or bacon, diced

Olive oil

Salt and pepper to taste

Fresh herbs like rosemary or bay leaves

Instructions

Making the Pisarei:

Mix the bread crumbs, flour, and a pinch of salt in a bowl. Gradually add water, mixing until a firm dough forms. Knead the dough until it's smooth and elastic.

Shape the Pisarei:

Take small pieces of dough and roll them into tiny oblong shapes, similar to small beans or chickpeas. Set aside on a floured surface to prevent sticking.

Making the Fasò (Bean Sauce):

In a large pan, heat olive oil over medium heat. Sauté onion, carrot, celery, and garlic (and pancetta, if using) until soft and fragrant. Add the Borlotti beans and crushed tomatoes to the pan. Season with salt, pepper, and add herbs. Simmer the sauce for about 30 minutes, letting the flavors meld together.

Bring a large pot of salted water to a boil. Cook the pisarei in batches until they float to the top, indicating they are done (about 2-3 minutes). Drain and add them to the bean sauce. Gently mix the cooked pisarei into the bean sauce, letting them absorb some of the flavors for a few minutes. Serve the pisarei e fasò hot, garnished with fresh herbs or grated Parmesan cheese if desired.

Cappelletti in Brodo di Cappone
Cappelletti in Capon Broth

Ingredients

For the Pasta Dough:
400 grams (about 3 1/3 cups) all-purpose flour
4 large eggs

For the Cappelletti Filling:
200 grams (about 7 ounces) mixed ground meat (pork, beef, and/or veal)
100 grams (about 3.5 ounces) grated Parmigiano Reggiano cheese
1 egg
Nutmeg, salt, and pepper to taste
Lemon zest (optional)
A pinch of salt

For the Brodo di Cappone (Capon Broth):
1 whole capon or large chicken, cleaned and gutted
1 onion, quartered
2 carrots, halved
2 celery stalks, halved
Salt and whole peppercorns
Fresh herbs (like parsley and thyme)
Water

Instructions

Making the Capon Broth:
In a large pot, place the capon or chicken, onion, carrots, celery, salt, peppercorns, and herbs. Fill the pot with water until all ingredients are submerged. Bring to a boil, then reduce to a simmer. Skim any foam that rises to the surface. Simmer for about 3-4 hours.
The longer it simmers, the richer the broth will be.
Strain the broth and keep it hot for serving.
The capon meat can be used in other dishes or as a filling.

Making the Cappelletti:
Mix the ground meat, grated cheese, egg, nutmeg, salt, pepper, and lemon zest in a bowl. Set aside.

Make the Pasta Dough:
On a clean surface, make a mound of flour with a well in the center. Crack the eggs into the well and add a pinch of salt. Gradually mix the flour into the eggs until a dough forms. Knead the dough until smooth. Let it rest for 30 minutes. Roll the dough into thin sheets. Cut into small squares (about 5 cm or 2 inches). Place a small amount of filling in the center of each square. Fold the dough into a triangle, then wrap the longer points around your finger and press to seal, forming the cappelletti shape. Bring the capon broth to a gentle boil. Cook the cappelletti in the broth until they float to the top and the pasta is tender, about 3-4 minutes. Serve the cappelletti in warm bowls of capon broth. Optionally, sprinkle with additional grated Parmigiano Reggiano.

Tuscany

A tour of Toscana (Tuscany), a region in central Italy known for its picturesque landscapes, rich art history, and culinary excellence, offers a quintessential Italian experience. Here's a description of what a tour through Tuscany might include:

Day 1: Arrival in Florence

Begin your journey in Florence, the capital of Tuscany, renowned for its Renaissance art and architecture. Visit the historic center, seeing the Duomo, the Baptistery, and Giotto's Bell Tower. Explore the Uffizi Gallery and the Accademia Gallery, home to Michelangelo's David.

Day 2: More of Florence

Spend another day in Florence exploring other notable sites such as the Palazzo Vecchio, the Ponte Vecchio, and the Pitti Palace.
Stroll through the Boboli Gardens and enjoy the panoramic view from Piazzale Michelangelo. In the evening, savor Florentine steak or other local specialties.

Day 3: The Chianti Region

Travel through the Chianti region, famous for its wine and scenic beauty. Visit wineries to taste Chianti Classico wines and olive oil, and explore small charming towns like Greve and Castellina in Chianti. Enjoy the rolling hills and vineyard landscapes of the Tuscan countryside.

Day 4: Siena and San Gimignano

Visit Siena, known for its medieval streets and the Piazza del Campo, where the Palio horse race is held. Explore the Siena Cathedral and the Museo dell'Opera. Head to San Gimignano, a UNESCO World Heritage site known for its tower houses and well-preserved medieval architecture.

Day 5: Pisa and Lucca

Travel to Pisa to see the iconic Leaning Tower, the Cathedral, and the Baptistery in the Piazza dei Miracoli. In the afternoon, visit Lucca, a city encircled by Renaissance walls, known for its cobblestone streets and rich history.
Explore Lucca's charming old town and visit landmarks like the Cathedral of San Martino and the Guinigi Tower.

Day 6: The Tuscan Countryside – Val d'Orcia

Explore the Val d'Orcia, another UNESCO World Heritage site, known for its quintessential Tuscan landscape of rolling hills and cypress trees. Visit picturesque towns like Pienza, known for its Pecorino cheese, and Montalcino, famous for Brunello di Montalcino wine.
Enjoy the region's natural hot springs, like those in Bagno Vignoni or Bagni San Filippo.

Day 7: Departure from Florence

Spend your last day in Florence for any final sightseeing or shopping, perhaps buying local crafts or gourmet products. Depart from Florence's airport or train station.

Pappardelle

Homemade pasta from Toscana

Homemade pasta from Tuscany, a region in central Italy known for its rich culinary traditions, is characterized by simple, rustic dishes that use high-quality local ingredients. Here are some key types of pasta and dishes typical of Tuscany:

Pappardelle: Wide, flat ribbons of pasta, typically served with hearty sauces. In Tuscany, pappardelle is often paired with rich, meaty sauces, particularly wild boar (cinghiale) or hare (lepre) ragù.

Tagliatelle: Similar to pappardelle but slightly narrower, tagliatelle is another popular pasta in Tuscany. It's commonly served with traditional meat sauces or with a simple sauce of butter and truffles, especially in areas where truffles are abundant.

Tortelli: These are stuffed pasta similar to ravioli. In Tuscany, tortelli is often filled with ricotta and spinach or with potato and served with a meat ragù or a butter and sage sauce.

Pici: A type of hand-rolled pasta similar to thick spaghetti, originating from the province of Siena. Pici is often served with garlic-heavy sauces, like aglione, or with bread crumbs and anchovies.

Testaroli: A unique and traditional Italian dish, particularly from the Lunigiana region in Northern Tuscany. This dish, often described as the oldest form of pasta, strikes an intriguing balance between pasta and pancake.

Pici all'Aglione
Pici with Garlic Sauce

Ingredients

For the Pici Pasta:
400 gr. (about 3 1/3 cups) of all-purpose flour
Warm water (as needed, usually about 200 ml)
A pinch of salt

For the Aglione Sauce:
4-6 cloves of garlic (or more, to taste)
800 grams (about 28 ounces) of ripe tomatoes or canned peeled tomatoes
Extra-virgin olive oil
Red pepper flakes (to taste)
Salt (to taste)
Fresh basil leaves (optional)

Instructions

Making Pici Pasta:
Mix the flour and salt in a bowl. Gradually add warm water, kneading until you have a smooth, firm dough. Divide the dough into small pieces. Roll each piece into long, thin ropes, about the thickness of a pencil.

Cook the Pasta:
Bring a large pot of salted water to a boil. Cook the pici until al dente (usually about 10-15 minutes).

Making Aglione Sauce:
Peel and finely slice (or crush) the garlic.
In a pan, heat a generous amount of olive oil.
Add the garlic and red pepper flakes, cooking until the garlic is golden (not burnt).
Add the tomatoes (crushed or chopped) to the pan. Season with salt. Cook on low heat for about 30 minutes, until the sauce thickens. You can add fresh basil for extra flavor. Once the sauce is ready, toss the cooked and drained pici in the sauce.

Pappardelle al Ragù di Cinta Senese

Pappardelle with Cinta Senese Ragù

Ingredients

For Homemade Pappardelle:
400 gr. of all-purpose flour
4 large eggs
A pinch of salt
A drizzle of olive oil

For the Cinta Senese Ragù:
500 grams of Cinta Senese Pork
(or a high-quality pork substitute), minced
Onion, Carrot, Celery: 1 of each, finely chopped
Garlic: 1 clove, minced
Red Wine: 1 cup (preferably a Tuscan variety)
Tomato Paste: 2 tablespoons
400 gr. of crushed tomatoes
1 Bay Leaf
Salt and pepper, to taste
Olive oil, for cooking

Instructions

Making Homemade Pappardelle:
On a clean surface, make a mound with the flour and create a well in the center. Crack the eggs into the well, add a pinch of salt and a drizzle of olive oil. Gradually mix the flour into the eggs until a dough forms. Knead for about 10 minutes until smooth and elastic. Wrap in cling film and let it rest for 30 minutes. Divide the dough into sections. Roll out each section to a thin sheet (about 1-2mm thick). Use a knife to cut the sheets into wide strips (about 2-3 cm wide). Hang the strips to dry slightly while you prepare the ragù.

Making the Ragù:
In a large pan, heat olive oil over medium heat. Add the onion, carrot, celery, and garlic, cooking until softened. Increase heat, add the pork, and cook until browned. Deglaze with Wine, add the red wine and let it reduce slightly. Stir in tomato paste and crushed tomatoes. Add bay leaf, salt, and pepper.
Lower heat and let it simmer for 2-3 hours, stirring occasionally. Add water if it gets too thick.
Bring a large pot of salted water to a boil. Cook the pappardelle until al dente, usually about 3-4 minutes. Drain: Reserve a cup of pasta water and drain the rest. Toss the pappardelle with the ragù, adding reserved pasta water if needed. Plate and garnish with grated Parmesan cheese and fresh herbs, if desired.

Pasta e Ceci
Pasta and Chickpeas

Ingredients

For Homemade Maltagliati:
200 gr. of all-purpose flour
2 large Eggs
A pinch of Salt
Water (as needed)
For the Soup:
250 gr. dried chickpeas (soaked overnight)
1 bay leaf
Salt (to taste)
60 ml Olive Oil
1 onion (chopped)
2 garlic cloves (minced)
1 carrot (chopped)
1 celery stalk (chopped)
400 gr. of crushed tomatoes
1000 ml of vegetable broth (or as needed)
5 gr. of rosemary (chopped)
5 gr. of thyme (chopped)
Salt and pepper (to taste)
Fresh Parsley (for garnish, chopped)

Instructions

Prepare the Chickpeas:
Soak chickpeas overnight in water.
Drain and cook in fresh water with a bay leaf and salt until tender (about 1-2 hours). Drain and set aside.
Making Homemade Maltagliati:
Place flour on a flat surface, make a well in the center, and crack the eggs into it. Add a pinch of salt. Gradually incorporate flour and eggs, adding water if necessary, to form a dough. Knead until smooth. Let rest for 30 minutes. Roll out the dough thinly and cut into irregular, diamond like shapes.
Making the Soup:
Heat olive oil in a large pot. Add onion, garlic, carrot, and celery. Cook until softened. Add crushed tomatoes, rosemary, and thyme. Cook for a few minutes. Pour in vegetable broth and bring to a boil. Simmer for 15 minutes.
Add cooked chickpeas. Continue simmering.
Bring a pot of salted water to boil. Cook maltagliati until al dente. Drain and add to the soup. Cook together briefly.
Adjust seasoning with salt and pepper.
Serve, garnishing with chopped fresh parsley.

Testaroli della Lunigiana al Pesto
Testaroli della Lunigiana with Pesto

Ingredients

For the Testaroli:
200 gr. All-Purpose Flour
400 ml Water
Salt (to taste)
Olive Oil (for the pan)

For the Pesto:
50 gr. of fresh basil leaves
30 gr. pine nuts
1 garlic clove
60 ml olive oil
30 gr. grated parmesan cheese
15 gr. grated pecorino cheese
Salt (to taste)

Instructions

Making the Testaroli:
Whisk together flour, water, and a pinch of salt to form a smooth, thin batter. Lightly oil a flat griddle or non-stick pan and heat over medium heat.

Pour a small amount of batter into the pan, spreading it to form a thin layer (like a crepe). Cook until the bottom is lightly browned, then flip and cook the other side.

Repeat with remaining batter. Once cooled, cut the testaroli into diamond or square shapes.

Making the Pesto:
In a food processor or mortar and pestle, blend basil, pine nuts, and garlic. Slowly add olive oil, blending until smooth. Stir in the Parmesan and Pecorino cheese. Season with salt.

Bring a pot of salted water to a boil. Cook the testaroli for just a few minutes until they rise to the surface.

Remove with a slotted spoon and drain. Toss the testaroli with the pesto sauce in a large bowl.

Umbria

A tour of Umbria, a region in central Italy known for its medieval hill towns, dense forests, and local cuisine, offers a serene and culturally rich experience. Known as the "green heart of Italy," Umbria is less touristy than its neighbor Tuscany, but just as enchanting.

Day 1: Arrival in Perugia

Begin your journey in Perugia, the capital of Umbria. Explore the historic center with its medieval streets, visiting the Fontana Maggiore and the Perugia Cathedral. Visit the National Gallery of Umbria and learn about the region's art history. Enjoy a dinner featuring Umbrian specialties, perhaps trying some local truffles.

Day 2: Assisi and its Spiritual Heritage

Travel to Assisi, the birthplace of St. Francis. Visit the Basilica of St. Francis, a UNESCO World Heritage site, renowned for its Giotto frescoes. Explore other significant sites like the Basilica of Santa Chiara and the Roman Temple of Minerva. Wander through the medieval streets and enjoy the peaceful ambiance.

Day 3: Spoleto and Montefalco

Head to Spoleto, known for its historic sites like the Spoleto Cathedral and the Rocca Albornoziana fortress.

In the afternoon, visit Montefalco, famous for its Sagrantino wine. Enjoy a wine tasting at a local vineyard.

Explore the town's charming streets and visit the Church of Saint Francis with its frescoes by Benozzo Gozzoli.

Day 4: Gubbio and its Ancient History

Visit Gubbio, one of the oldest towns in Umbria, with well-preserved medieval architecture.

See the Roman Theater, the Palazzo dei Consoli, and take a funicular to the Basilica of Saint Ubaldo. Enjoy local cuisine, such as wild boar or the traditional crescia flatbread.

Day 5: Todi and Orvieto

Travel to Todi, a picturesque medieval town perched on a hill. Visit the Todi Cathedral and the Piazza del Popolo.

In the afternoon, head to Orvieto. Visit the stunning Orvieto Cathedral, famous for its façade and Signorelli's frescoes.

Explore the underground city of Orvieto with its tunnels and caves.

Day 6: The Marmore Waterfall and Lake Trasimeno

Visit the Marmore Waterfall, one of the tallest waterfalls in Europe, located near Terni. Spend the afternoon at Lake Trasimeno, the largest lake in central Italy. Enjoy a boat trip to one of the islands or relax by the lakeside.

Day 7: Departure from Perugia

Spend your last day in Perugia, perhaps visiting the Perugina Chocolate Factory for a tour and tasting.

Depart from Perugia's airport or train station.

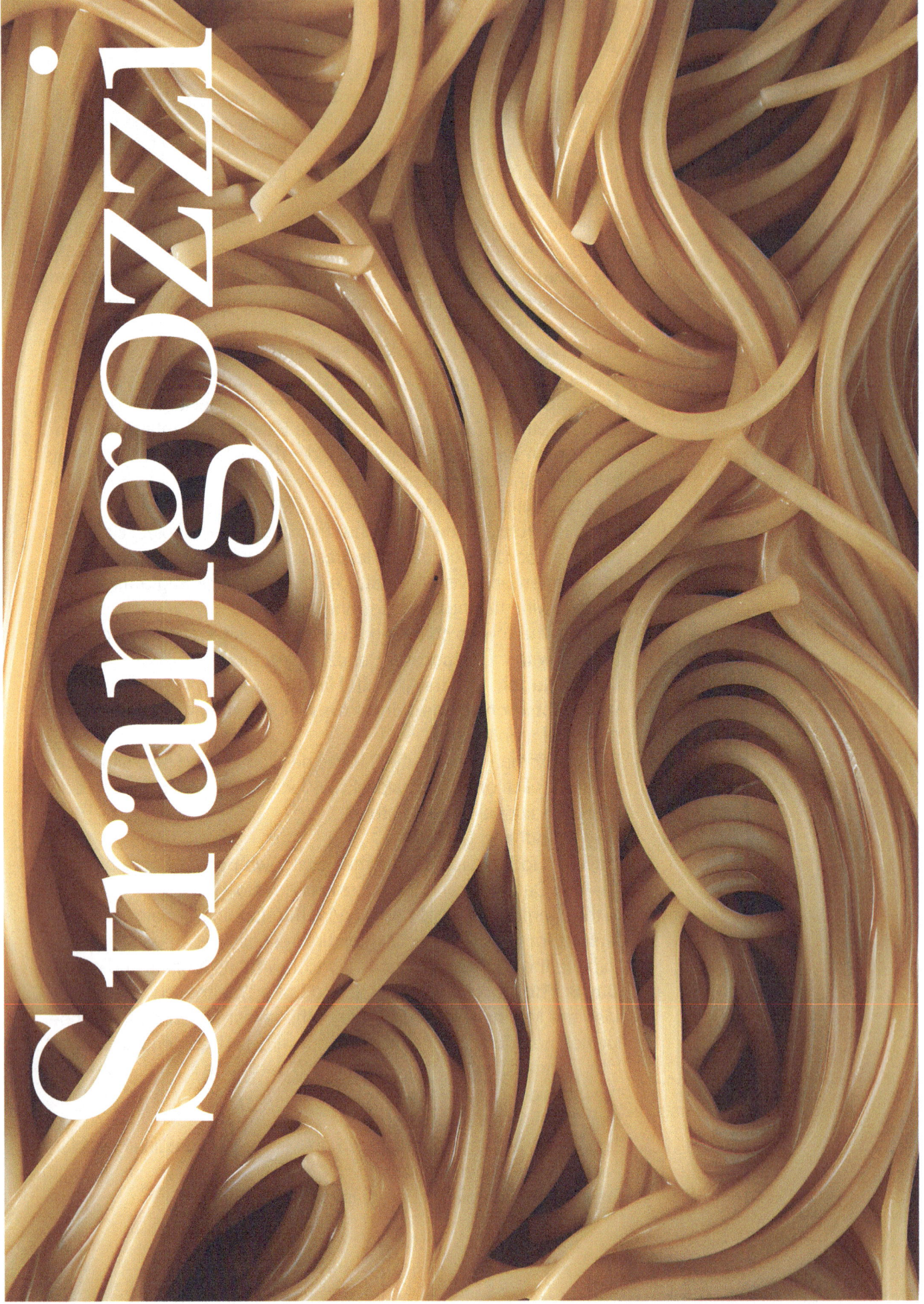

Strangozzi

Homemade pasta from Umbria

Homemade pasta from Umbria, a region in central Italy renowned for its rich culinary traditions, reflects the simplicity and rusticity typical of Umbrian cuisine. Here are some key types of pasta and dishes typical of Umbria:

Strangozzi or Stringozzi: This is a traditional Umbrian pasta, similar to spaghetti but thicker and slightly chewier. Made with only flour and water, strangozzi is often served with black truffles (tartufo nero), which are abundant in Umbria, or with a hearty tomato and garlic sauce.

Umbricelli: Similar to strangozzi but even thicker, umbricelli is a hand-rolled pasta typically served with a meat ragù or a truffle sauce. It's a rustic pasta that embodies the heartiness of Umbrian cuisine.

Pappardelle: Wide, flat ribbons of egg pasta, pappardelle is common in Umbria as in other regions of Italy. In Umbria, they are often served with game meat sauces, such as wild boar or hare, reflecting the region's strong hunting tradition.

Ciriole: A thicker version of tagliatelle, made with flour, water, and sometimes eggs. This pasta is typically served with a simple sauce made from fresh tomatoes and basil or with a ragù.

Strangozzi alla Spoletina
Strangozzi Spoleto-Style

Ingredients

For the Strangozzi:
400 gr. of all-purpose flour
200 ml of water (lukewarm)
A pinch of salt
olive oil (for the dough)
For the Sauce (Alla Spoletina):
400 gr. of crushed tomatoes
2 garlic cloves (minced)
60 ml of olive oil
A handful of fresh basil leaves
Salt and pepper (to taste)
Grated pecorino cheese (for serving)

Instructions

Making the Strangozzi:
Combine the flour, salt, and a drizzle of olive oil in a large bowl. Gradually add the lukewarm water, mixing until a dough begins to form. Turn the dough onto a floured surface and knead until smooth and elastic, about 10 minutes. Cover the dough with a cloth and let it rest for about 30 minutes. Divide the dough into small portions. Roll each portion into long, thin ropes (about the thickness of a pencil). Cut the ropes into pieces about 30 cm in length. Cook the stringozzi in a large pot of boiling salted water until they float to the surface and are al dente.

Making the Sauce (Alla Spoletina):
In a saucepan, heat the olive oil over medium heat. Add the minced garlic and cook until fragrant but not browned. Stir in the crushed tomatoes, and season with salt and pepper. Let the sauce simmer gently for about 15-20 minutes, allowing the flavors to meld. Add the fresh basil towards the end of cooking. Once the stringozzi are cooked, drain them, reserving a little pasta water. Add the stringozzi to the sauce, tossing gently. Use the reserved pasta water to adjust the consistency of the sauce if needed.

Umbricelli al Rancetto
Umbricelli with Rancetto Sauce

Ingredients

For the Umbricelli:
400 gr. of all-purpose flour
200 ml. of water (lukewarm)
A pinch of salt

For the Rancetto Sauce:
150 gr. of pancetta (diced)
400 gr. of crushed tomatoes
1 onion (finely chopped)
2 cloves of garlic (minced)
30 ml. of olive oil
A handful of fresh basil leaves
Salt and pepper (to taste)
Grated pecorino cheese (for serving)

Instructions

Making the Umbricelli:

Mix the flour and a pinch of salt in a large bowl.
Gradually add lukewarm water, stirring until a dough begins to form. Turn the dough onto a floured surface and knead until smooth and elastic, about 10 minutes. Cover the dough and let it rest for about 30 minutes. Divide the dough into small portions. Roll each portion by hand on a floured surface to create long, thick strands, similar to thick spaghetti. Boil the umbricelli in salted water until they are al dente.

Making the Rancetto Sauce:

In a pan, cook the diced pancetta until it starts to brown. Add olive oil, chopped onion, and minced garlic to the pan. Cook until the onion is soft. Stir in the crushed tomatoes. Season with salt and pepper. Let the sauce simmer for about 15-20 minutes. Add the fresh basil towards the end. Once the umbricelli are cooked, drain them, reserving a bit of the pasta water. Add the umbricelli to the sauce, tossing to coat. Use the reserved pasta water to adjust the sauce consistency if needed.

Ciriole alla Norcina
Ciriole with Norcina Sauce

Ingredients

For the Ciriole:
400 gr. of all-purpose flour
200 ml. of water (lukewarm)
A pinch of salt
For the Norcina Sauce:
250 gr. of pork sausage (casings removed)
200 gr. of heavy cream
1 clove of garlic (minced)
30 ml of olive oil
50 gr. of grated Parmesan cheese
10 gr. of black truffle
(finely grated or truffle paste, optional)
salt and pepper (to taste)

Instructions

Making the Ciriole:
In a large bowl, mix the flour and salt. Gradually add lukewarm water, stirring until a dough forms.
Knead on a floured surface until smooth and elastic, about 10 minutes. Let the dough rest, covered, for about 30 minutes. Divide the dough into smaller pieces.
Roll each piece into long, thick strands. Boil the ciriole in salted water until al dente.
Making the Norcina Sauce:
In a pan, cook the sausage in olive oil over medium heat, breaking it into small pieces. Add minced garlic to the sausage and cook until fragrant. Lower the heat and add the heavy cream, stirring well. Add grated Parmesan, truffle (if using), salt, and pepper. Cook until the sauce thickens slightly. Once the ciriole is cooked, drain it, saving a bit of the pasta water.
Mix with Sauce: Add the ciriole to the sauce, tossing to combine. Use the reserved pasta water to adjust the sauce consistency if needed.

Marche

A tour of Marche, a region in central Italy known for its rolling hills, Renaissance art, and beautiful Adriatic coastline, offers a blend of cultural, historical, and natural experiences.

Day 1: Arrival in Ancona

Begin your journey in Ancona, the capital of the Marche region. Visit the Cathedral of San Ciriaco, located on a hilltop with panoramic views of the Adriatic Sea. Explore the historic city center and enjoy a seafood dinner in one of the local restaurants.

Day 2: The Conero Riviera

Explore the Riviera del Conero, known for its beautiful beaches and dramatic cliffs. Visit picturesque towns like Sirolo and Numana, enjoying their beaches and hiking trails. Sample local wines, such as Rosso Conero, in one of the many vineyards in the area.

Day 3: Urbino, a Renaissance Gem

Travel to Urbino, a UNESCO World Heritage Site, famous for its Renaissance heritage. Visit the Palazzo Ducale, home to the Galleria Nazionale delle Marche, showcasing works by artists like Raphael and Piero della Francesca. Explore the historic city center with its well-preserved Renaissance architecture.

Day 4: The Caves of Frasassi

Visit the Grotte di Frasassi, one of the most spectacular cave systems in Europe. Take a guided tour of the caves, admiring the incredible stalactites and stalagmites. In the afternoon, visit the nearby medieval town of Fabriano, known for its paper-making heritage.

Day 5: Ascoli Piceno and its Piazzas

Head to Ascoli Piceno, renowned for its beautiful piazzas, like Piazza del Popolo and Piazza Arringo.
Visit the Cathedral of Sant'Emidio and see the historic Caffè Meletti, famous for its Art Nouveau interior.
Try local specialties, such as olive all'ascolana (stuffed, fried olives).

Day 6: The Sibillini Mountains and Macerata

Explore the Sibillini Mountains National Park, offering stunning natural landscapes and hiking opportunities. In the afternoon, visit Macerata, known for its open-air opera festival and the Sferisterio arena.
Enjoy a stroll through the town's historic center and visit the Palazzo Ricci art gallery.

Day 7: Departure from Ancona

Spend your last day in Ancona, perhaps visiting the Arch of Trajan or the Museo Archeologico Nazionale delle Marche. Enjoy a final walk along the port or a relaxing day at one of the nearby beaches. Depart from Ancona's airport or train station.

Maccheroncini di Campofilone

Homemade pasta from Marche

Homemade pasta from Marche, a region in central Italy, reflects the area's culinary traditions, combining influences from both the inland mountains and the Adriatic coast. The pasta of Marche is characterized by its variety and the use of simple, locally sourced ingredients.

Maccheroncini di Campofilone: Perhaps the most famous pasta from Marche, these are very thin, egg-based noodles similar to angel hair pasta. They are traditionally made with a high ratio of eggs to flour, creating a delicate texture. Often served with a simple sauce, they highlight the quality of the pasta itself.

Vincisgrassi: This is the Marchigian version of lasagna and is richer and more elaborate. It typically includes layers of flat pasta sheets with a meat sauce (ragù), béchamel sauce, and various cheeses. The meat sauce often contains chicken livers, giving it a distinctive flavor.

Passatelli: Made from a mixture of breadcrumbs, eggs, grated Parmesan cheese, and lemon zest, passatelli are pushed through a passatelli iron or potato ricer to form thick, short, spaghetti-like noodles. They are typically served in broth, making a hearty and comforting dish.

Cappelletti: Similar to tortellini, cappelletti are small, stuffed pasta shapes. In Marche, they are traditionally filled with a mixture of meats, such as pork, beef, or chicken, along with Parmesan cheese. They are often served in capon broth.

Maccheroncini di Campofilone al Ragù Marchigiano

Maccheroncini di Campofilone with Marchigiano Ragù

Ingredients

For the Maccheroncini di Campofilone:
400 gr. of '00' flour (high-quality, fine flour)
8 large eggs

For the Ragù Marchigiano:
150 gr. of beef, minced
150 gr. of pork, minced
100 gr. of chicken livers, finely chopped (optional)
50 ml of olive oil
1 onion, finely chopped
1 carrot, finely chopped
1 celery stalk, finely chopped
150 ml of dry white wine
400 gr. of crushed tomatoes
Salt and pepper (to taste)
Water or broth (as needed)

Instructions

Making the Maccheroncini di Campofilone:
Mix the '00' flour with the eggs until a smooth dough forms. Knead until elastic. Cover the dough and let it rest for about 30 minutes. Roll the dough into very thin sheets (almost transparent). Once the sheets are dry but still pliable, roll them up and slice thinly to create maccheroncini. Unroll the maccheroncini and let them dry completely.

Making the Ragù Marchigiano:
In a large pot, heat the olive oil. Add the onion, carrot, and celery, and cook until they begin to soften. Add the minced beef and pork, and chicken livers if using. Cook until browned. Pour in the white wine, scraping up any browned bits from the bottom of the pot. Stir in the crushed tomatoes, salt, and pepper. Allow the sauce to simmer gently for at least 2 hours, adding water or broth as necessary to keep it from drying out.

Bring a large pot of salted water to a boil.

Cook the maccheroncini until al dente, usually just a few minutes due to their thinness. Reserve a cup of pasta water, then drain the pasta. Add the maccheroncini to the ragù, tossing gently. Use the reserved pasta water to adjust the consistency if needed.

Passatelli in Brodo
Passatelli in Broth

Ingredients

For the Passatelli:
200 gr. of breadcrumbs
100 gr. of grated Parmesan cheese
3 large eggs
Lemon zest (from 1 lemon)
Nutmeg (a pinch)
Salt and pepper (to taste)
For the Brodo (Broth):
1500 ml of chicken or beef broth
1 carrot
1 onion
1 celery stalk
Salt (to taste)

Instructions

Making the Brodo:
In a large pot, combine the chicken or beef broth, carrot, onion, and celery. Bring to a boil. Reduce the heat and let it simmer for about 30 minutes to allow the flavors to infuse. Season with salt as needed. Strain the broth to remove the vegetables and keep it warm.

Making the Passatelli:
In a bowl, combine the breadcrumbs, grated Parmesan, lemon zest, nutmeg, salt, and pepper.
Add Eggs: Mix in the eggs until a firm dough forms. If the mixture is too dry, add a little more egg.
Using a passatelli maker or a potato ricer with large holes, press the dough directly into the simmering broth. They will cook quickly and float to the surface when done, usually in about 1-2 minutes. Ladle the broth and passatelli into bowls. This dish is traditionally enjoyed hot, especially during colder months, offering a comforting and hearty meal.

Pappardelle al Ragù di Anatra
Pappardelle with Duck Sauce

Ingredients

For the Pappardelle:
300 gr. of '00' flour (or all-purpose flour)
3 large eggs

For the Duck Ragù:
500 gr of duck meat (legs or breast), cut into small pieces
50 ml of olive oil
1 onion, finely chopped
1 carrot, finely chopped
1 celery stalk, finely chopped
2 cloves of garlic, minced
150 ml of red wine
400 gr. of crushed tomatoes
250 ml of chicken or duck broth
1 sprig of rosemary
1 sprig of thyme
Salt and pepper (to taste)

Instructions

Making the Pappardelle:
In a large bowl, combine the flour and eggs. Knead until a smooth, elastic dough forms. Let the dough rest, covered, for about 30 minutes. Roll the dough into thin sheets. Cut the sheets into wide strips to form pappardelle. Allow the pappardelle to dry slightly before cooking.

Making the Duck Ragù:
In a large pot, heat the olive oil. Brown the duck pieces, then remove and set aside. In the same pot, add onion, carrot, celery, and garlic. Cook until softened. Add the red wine, scraping up any browned bits from the bottom. Stir in the crushed tomatoes and broth. Return the duck to the pot. Add rosemary, thyme, salt, and pepper. Let the ragù simmer on low heat for about 2 hours, until the duck is tender. Bring a large pot of salted water to a boil.

Cook Pasta: Cook the pappardelle until al dente. Reserve some pasta water and then drain the pappardelle.

Add the pappardelle to the duck ragù, tossing gently. Use reserved pasta water to adjust the sauce consistency if needed.

Maccheroncini di Campofilone al Sugo di Calamari

Maccheroncini di Campofilone with Squid Sauce

Ingredients

For the Maccheroncini di Campofilone:
400 gr. of '00' flour (fine, high-quality flour)
8 large eggs

For the Calamari Sauce:
500 gr of calamari, cleaned and cut into rings
50 ml of olive oil
1 clove of garlic, minced
1 small onion, finely chopped
200 ml of white wine
400 gr of crushed tomatoes
Salt and pepper (to taste)
A handful of fresh parsley, chopped

Instructions

Making the Maccheroncini di Campofilone:

In a large bowl, mix the '00' flour with the eggs until a smooth dough forms. Knead until elastic. Cover and let the dough rest for about 30 minutes. Roll the dough into very thin sheets (almost transparent). Cut the sheets into thin strands to create maccheroncini.

Allow the maccheroncini to dry slightly before cooking.

Making the Calamari Sauce:

In a pan, heat olive oil over medium heat. Add garlic and onion, cooking until soft and fragrant.

Stir in the calamari rings and cook for a couple of minutes. Pour in the white wine and let it simmer until reduced by half. Stir in the crushed tomatoes.

Season with salt and pepper. Let the sauce simmer for about 20-30 minutes, until the calamari is tender and the sauce is flavorful. Add chopped parsley near the end of cooking. Bring a large pot of salted water to a boil.

Cook the maccheroncini until al dente, usually just a few minutes. Reserve a cup of pasta water, then drain the pasta. Add the maccheroncini to the calamari sauce, tossing gently. Use the reserved pasta water to adjust the sauce consistency if needed.

Lazio

A tour of Lazio, a central region of Italy known for its historical, cultural, and natural wonders, offers a journey through ancient history, Renaissance art, and beautiful landscapes.

Day 1: Arrival in Rome

Begin your journey in Rome, the capital city of Italy and Lazio.

Explore iconic landmarks such as the Colosseum, Roman Forum, and Pantheon. Stroll through the historic center, visiting the Trevi Fountain and Spanish Steps.

Day 2: Vatican City and Rome's Renaissance Art

Dedicate the day to Vatican City, visiting St. Peter's Basilica and the Vatican Museums, including the Sistine Chapel. In the afternoon, explore Rome's Renaissance and Baroque sites, like Piazza Navona and Campo de' Fiori.

Day 3: Ancient Ostia and the Roman Coast

Take a trip to Ostia Antica, an ancient port city of Rome, to see well-preserved ruins. Spend the afternoon at Ostia Lido, enjoying the beaches along the Tyrrhenian Sea. Enjoy seafood cuisine at a coastal restaurant.

Day 4: Tivoli's Villas and Gardens

Visit Tivoli, home to Villa d'Este, famous for its Renaissance gardens and fountains, and the ancient Villa Adriana (Hadrian's Villa), a UNESCO World Heritage site. Explore the charming streets of Tivoli and enjoy local culinary specialties.

Day 5: The Etruscan Heartland - Tarquinia and Cerveteri

Explore the Etruscan necropolises of Tarquinia and Cerveteri, both UNESCO World Heritage sites, known for their ancient tombs and frescoes. Visit the National Archaeological Museum of Tarquinia to see Etruscan artifacts.

Day 6: The Castelli Romani

Discover the Castelli Romani, a group of towns in the Alban Hills, known for their history, culture, and cuisine.

Visit Castel Gandolfo, the Pope's summer residence, and enjoy the views of Lake Albano. Sample local wines and dishes, like porchetta, in the town of Frascati.

Day 7: Departure from Rome

Spend your last day in Rome visiting any missed sites or doing some last-minute shopping.

Sample more of Rome's culinary delights, from classic pasta dishes to gelato.mDepart from Rome's international airport or train stations.

Fettuccine

Homemade pasta from Lazio

Lazio boasts a rich culinary tradition with several distinctive types of homemade pasta. These pastas are deeply rooted in the region's history and culture.

Fettuccine: Similar to tagliatelle, but slightly thicker and wider, fettuccine is one of the most famous pastas from the Lazio region. Traditionally, it's made with egg and flour and is often served with ragù or a hearty meat sauce.

Bucatini: This long, thick pasta with a hole running through the center (similar to thick spaghetti but with a hollow center) is a staple in Roman cuisine. Bucatini all'Amatriciana, a dish with a sauce made from guanciale (cured pork cheek), Pecorino cheese, and tomato, is particularly renowned.

Gnocchi di Semola: This is a unique Roman specialty. Unlike the more commonly known potato gnocchi, these are made from semolina flour, milk, eggs, and cheese, often baked with a savory sauce and more cheese.

Pappardelle: While pappardelle is found throughout Italy, in Lazio, it's often served with game meat sauces, particularly hare (lepre) or wild boar (cinghiale).

Cannelloni: Originated as a Roman dish, cannelloni are large pasta tubes that are typically filled with ricotta and spinach or with a meat filling, covered in a béchamel sauce, and baked until golden.

Tonnarelli: Similar to spaghetti but slightly thicker and square-cut, tonnarelli is often served with cacio e pepe (cheese and pepper), a quintessential Roman dish.

Bucatini all'Amatriciana
Bucatini in the Style of Amatrice

Ingredients

For the Pasta:
400 gr. of durum wheat semolina flour (or '00' flour)
200 ml of water (lukewarm)
A pinch of salt

For the Amatriciana Sauce:
150 gr. of guanciale
(if unavailable, substitute with pancetta)
400 gr. of crushed tomatoes
1 red chili pepper (or chili flakes to taste)
50 gr. of grated Pecorino Romano cheese
30 ml of olive oil
Salt (to taste)

Instructions

Making the Bucatini:
In a large bowl, mix the flour and salt. Gradually add lukewarm water, stirring until a dough forms.
Knead: Knead on a floured surface until smooth and elastic, about 10 minutes. Let the dough rest, covered, for about 30 minutes.

Forming Bucatini:
Use a pasta machine or a hand-held pasta extruder to form the dough into long, hollow strands typical of bucatini.
Boil the bucatini in salted water until al dente.

Making the Amatriciana Sauce:
In a large pan, heat olive oil. Add guanciale (or pancetta) and cook until it starts to crisp. Stir in the crushed tomatoes. Add the red chili pepper or chili flakes. Simmer for about 15-20 minutes. Adjust seasoning with salt, keeping in mind that guanciale and Pecorino are salty. Once the bucatini is cooked, drain it, saving a bit of the pasta water. Mix with Sauce: Add the bucatini to the sauce, tossing to combine. Use the reserved pasta water to adjust the sauce consistency if needed.

Tonnarelli Cacio e Pepe
Tonnarelli with Cheese and Pepper

Ingredients

For the Tonnarelli:

400 gr. of '00' flour (or a mix of '00' and semolina flour)

4 large eggs

Water (as needed, if the dough is too dry)

For the Cacio e Pepe Sauce:

200 gr. of Pecorino Romano cheese, finely grated

Freshly ground black pepper (to taste)

Salt (for the pasta water)

Instructions

Making the Tonnarelli:

In a bowl, mix the flour with the eggs. Add a little water if necessary to bring the dough together. Knead the dough on a floured surface until smooth and elastic. Cover the dough and let it rest for about 30 minutes.

Roll the dough into a thin sheet and cut it into square spaghetti-like strands (tonnarelli). Cook the tonnarelli in a large pot of boiling salted water until al dente.

Making the Cacio e Pepe Sauce:

In a bowl, mix the grated Pecorino Romano with enough cold water to make a creamy paste. Set aside.

Once the tonnarelli is cooked, reserve a cup of the pasta water before draining. Return the cooked pasta to the pot over low heat. Add the cheese mixture and a generous amount of freshly ground black pepper. Toss the pasta, adding reserved pasta water as needed to create a creamy sauce that coats the tonnarelli. Plate the tonnarelli cacio e pepe immediately, adding more black pepper on top if desired.

Fettuccine alla Papalina
Fettuccine in the Papal Style

Ingredients

For the Fettuccine:
300 gr. of '00' flour (or all-purpose flour)
3 large eggs

For the Papalina Sauce:
150 gr. of cooked ham, finely chopped
1 small onion, finely chopped
50 ml of olive oil
200 ml of heavy cream
2 large eggs
100 gr. of grated Parmesan cheese
Salt and pepper (to taste)
Optional addition of peas

Instructions

Making the Fettuccine:
In a large bowl, mix the flour and eggs until a smooth dough forms. Add a little water if the dough is too dry. Knead the dough on a floured surface until smooth and elastic. Let the dough rest, covered, for about 30 minutes. Rolling and Cutting: Roll out the dough into thin sheets, then cut into long, flat strips to make fettuccine. Boil the fettuccine in salted water until al dente.

Making the Papalina Sauce:
In a skillet, heat the olive oil. Add the onion and cook until translucent. Add the ham and peas, cook for a few minutes. In a bowl, whisk together the eggs, cream, and half of the grated Parmesan. Season with salt and pepper.
Drain the cooked fettuccine, reserving some pasta water. Add the fettuccine to the skillet with the ham and onion. Remove from heat, then quickly stir in the egg and cream mixture, tossing continuously to create a creamy sauce. Use the reserved pasta water as needed to adjust the consistency. Plate the fettuccine alla papalina and sprinkle with the remaining grated Parmesan.

Abruzzo

A tour of Abruzzo, Italy, offers a blend of picturesque landscapes, rich history, and exquisite culinary experiences. Here's a description of what such a tour might encompass:

Day 1: Arrival in Pescara

Start in Pescara, the largest city in Abruzzo. Explore the seafront promenade and visit the birthplace of the poet Gabriele D'Annunzio. Enjoy a seafood dinner at a local restaurant.

Day 2: The Coastal Charm

Visit the Trabocchi Coast, known for its unique fishing structures. Stop by the town of Vasto, with its beautiful beaches and historical center. Enjoy a lunch of "Brodetto di Pesce," a traditional fish stew.

Day 3: Into the Mountains - National Parks

Head towards the Majella National Park or Gran Sasso National Park. Enjoy hiking or guided nature walks to explore the flora and fauna. Visit a local agriturismo for a taste of authentic Abruzzese cuisine.

Day 4: Medieval Towns and Art

Explore the medieval town of Chieti, with its Roman ruins and museums. Visit the National Archaeological Museum of Abruzzo. In the evening, explore the charming streets and enjoy local wines and cheeses.

Day 5: Culinary Experiences in Abruzzo

Participate in a cooking class to learn how to make traditional Abruzzese dishes, including homemade pasta. Visit a local vineyard for a wine tasting session, featuring the renowned Montepulciano d'Abruzzo.

Day 6: Ancient Villages and Traditions

Explore the ancient village of Scanno, famous for its traditional jewelry and picturesque streets. Visit the nearby Lake Scanno for stunning views and relaxation. In the evening, enjoy traditional music and dance in a local festival or event.

Day 7: Farewell to Abruzzo

Spend your last day in Sulmona, known for its confetti (sugar-coated almonds) and beautiful medieval architecture. Visit the Sulmona Cathedral and stroll through the weekly market. Depart from Pescara or the nearest airport.

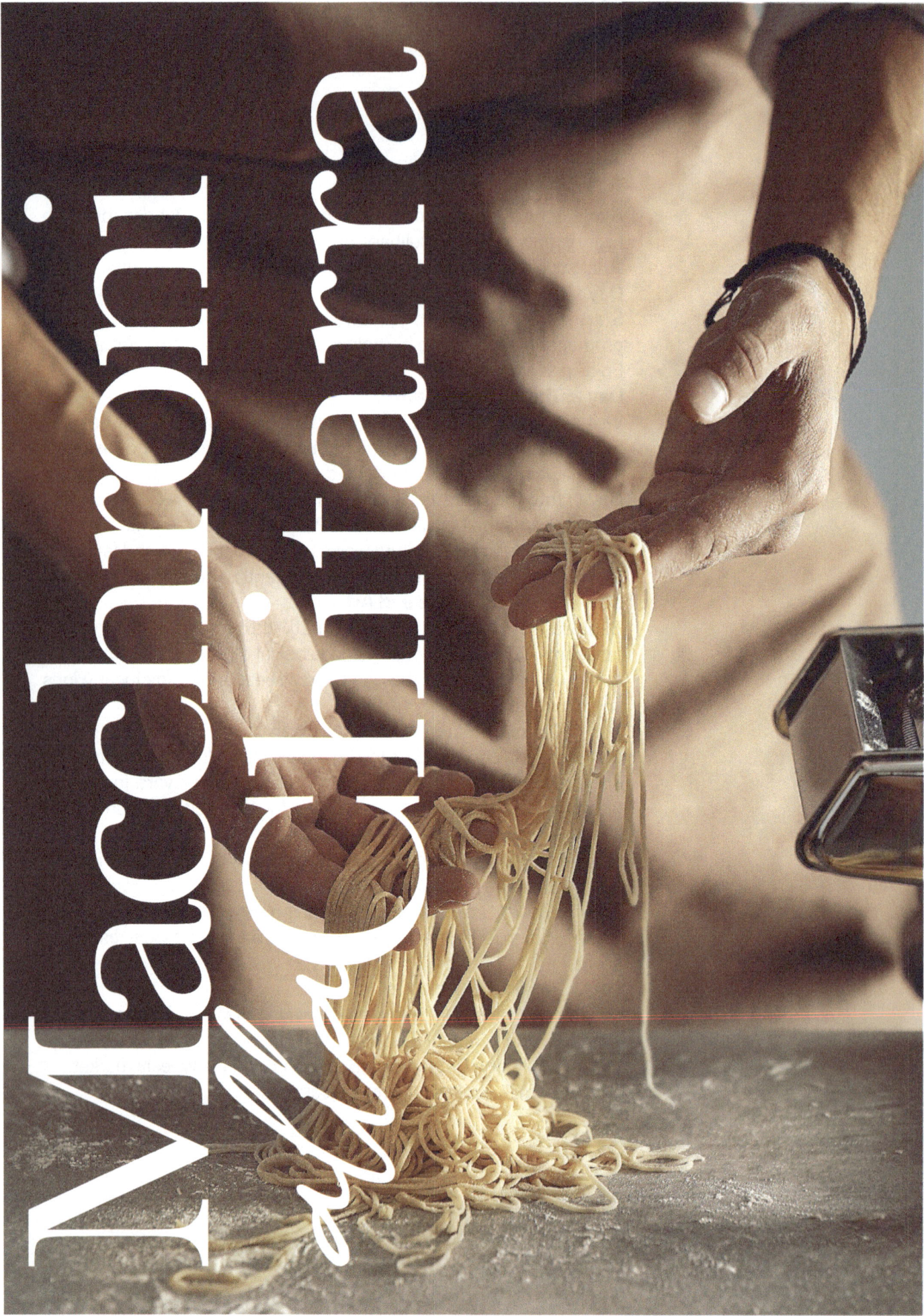
Maccchroni alla Chitarra

Homemade pasta from Abruzzo

Abruzzo, a region in central Italy, is known for its diverse and rich culinary traditions, including a variety of unique homemade pastas.

These pastas are integral to the region's culinary identity and showcase the simplicity and rusticity of Abruzzese cuisine.

Maccheroni alla Chitarra: This is perhaps the most famous pasta from Abruzzo. It's made by pressing sheets of pasta dough through a tool known as a 'chitarra' (guitar), which cuts the pasta into long, square-shaped strands. Traditionally, it's served with a hearty meat sauce or a simple tomato sauce.

Gnocchi Carrati: This unique variety of gnocchi, native to the mountains of Abruzzo, is made with a mixture of potatoes, pecorino cheese, and eggs, and it's often flavored with saffron. It's typically served with a pork ragu.

Sagne: Sagne refers to a type of pasta similar to tagliatelle but shorter and narrower. It's commonly combined with beans (fagioli) for a classic Abruzzese dish.

Scrippelle: These are thin crepes made from a simple batter of eggs, flour, and water. Scrippelle are often rolled up with grated pecorino cheese inside, and then served in chicken broth, in a dish known as "Scrippelle 'mbusse".

Ravioli Dolci: These are sweet ravioli, unique to Abruzzo, filled with a mixture of cocoa, cinnamon, and sometimes liqueur-soaked fruits. They're typically served during festive occasions.

Pasta alla Mugnaia: A traditional pasta from Elice, it's a single, long strand of thick pasta, sometimes several meters in length, made with only flour and water. It's often served with a simple tomato sauce and lots of pecorino cheese.

Fregnacce: Similar to lasagna, fregnacce are wide, flat strips of pasta layered with various sauces and ingredients, often baked in the oven.

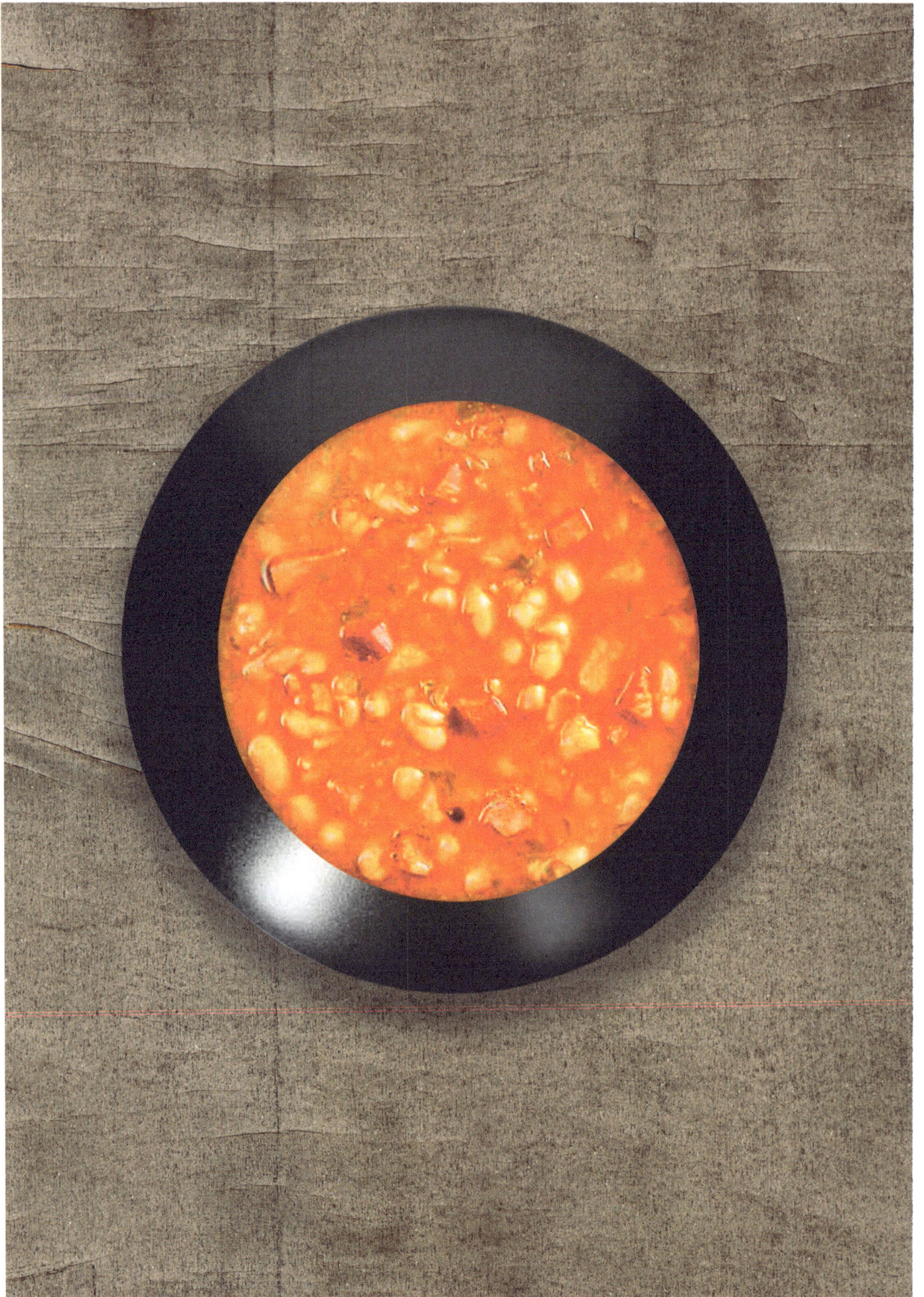

Sagne e Fagioli
Sagne and Beans

Ingredients

For the Sagne Pasta:
300 gr. of all-purpose flour
150 ml of water (approximately)
A pinch of salt

For the Beans:
250 gr. of dried cannellini beans or chickpeas (soaked overnight)
Water (for soaking and cooking)

For the Sauce:
50 ml of olive oil
1 onion, finely chopped
2 cloves of garlic, minced
400 gr. of crushed tomatoes
Salt and pepper (to taste)
A sprig of rosemary

Instructions

Prepare the Beans or Chickpeas:
Soak the cannellini beans or chickpeas overnight in plenty of water. Drain the beans, then cook in fresh water until tender, about 1-2 hours.

Making the Sagne Pasta:
In a large bowl, mix the flour and salt. Gradually add water, kneading until a firm dough forms. Let the dough rest, covered, for about 30 minutes. Roll out the dough thinly. Cut into narrow, short strips (about 5 cm long and 1 cm wide). Cook the sagne in boiling salted water until al dente.

Making the Sauce:
In a large pan, heat olive oil. Add onion and garlic, cooking until soft. Stir in the crushed tomatoes, rosemary, salt, and pepper. Simmer for about 15 minutes.

Add the cooked beans to the sauce. Let it simmer together for a few minutes. Once the sagne is cooked, drain and add it to the sauce with beans. Let the pasta and beans cook together briefly, so the flavors meld. Plate the sagne e fagioli, drizzling with a bit more olive oil if desired.

Maccheroni alla Chitarra con le Pallottoline alla Teramana

Maccheroni alla Chitarra with Teramana-style Meatballs

Ingredients

For the Maccheroni alla Chitarra:
400 gr. of '00' flour (or a mix of '00' and semolina flour)
4 large eggs

For the Pallottoline (Meatballs):
300 gr. of ground beef
100 gr. of ground pork
50 gr. of breadcrumbs
50 ml of milk
1 large egg
50 gr of grated Pecorino cheese
A handful of fresh parsley, chopped
Salt and pepper (to taste)

For the Sauce:
30 ml of olive oil
1 onion, finely chopped
2 cloves of garlic, minced
400 gr. of crushed tomatoes
Salt and pepper (to taste)
A pinch of sugar (optional)

Instructions

Making the Maccheroni alla Chitarra:
In a large bowl, combine the flour and eggs. Knead until a smooth, elastic dough forms. Let the dough rest, covered, for about 30 minutes.

Forming Maccheroni:
Use a traditional 'chitarra' frame or a pasta roller to roll out the dough and cut it into long, square spaghetti-like strands. Cook the maccheroni in boiling salted water until al dente.

Preparing the Pallottoline:
Combine Ingredients: In a bowl, mix the ground beef and pork, breadcrumbs soaked in milk, egg, grated Pecorino, parsley, salt, and pepper.

Form Meatballs: Shape the mixture into small meatballs, about the size of marbles. Fry the meatballs in olive oil until browned, then set aside.

In the same pan, add more olive oil if needed. Sauté onion and garlic until translucent. Stir in the crushed tomatoes, salt, pepper, and a pinch of sugar. Let the sauce simmer for about 15-20 minutes. Add the cooked meatballs to the sauce and let them simmer together for another 10 15 minutes. Once the maccheroni are cooked, drain them, saving a bit of the pasta water.

Add the maccheroni to the sauce with meatballs, tossing to combine. Use the reserved pasta water to adjust the sauce consistency if needed.

Pasta alla Mugnaia con Sugo di Carne
Pasta alla Mugnaia with Meat Sauce

Ingredients

For the Pasta alla Mugnaia:
500 gr of all-purpose flour
250 ml of water (approximately)
A pinch of salt

For the Abruzzese Meat Sauce:
300 gr of beef, cubed
200 gr of pork, cubed
100 gr of lamb, cubed (optional)
50 ml of olive oil
1 onion, finely chopped
2 cloves of garlic, minced
150 ml of red wine
400 gr of crushed tomatoes
Salt and pepper (to taste)
A sprig of rosemary
A sprig of thyme

Instructions

Making the Pasta alla Mugnaia:
In a large bowl, mix the flour and salt. Gradually add water, kneading until a firm, elastic dough forms. Let the dough rest for about 30 minutes. Divide the dough into smaller portions. Roll each portion by hand on a floured surface to create very long, thick strands, resembling thick spaghetti but much longer and slightly irregular. Cook the pasta in a large pot of boiling salted water until al dente.

Preparing the Abruzzese Meat Sauce:
In a large pot, heat olive oil over medium heat. Add the beef, pork, and lamb, browning the meat on all sides.
Add the chopped onion and minced garlic to the pot, cooking until the onion is translucent.
Deglaze: Pour in the red wine, allowing it to simmer and reduce slightly. Stir in the crushed tomatoes, rosemary, thyme, salt, and pepper. Let the sauce simmer on low heat for about 2 hours, until the meat is tender and the flavors are well combined. Once the pasta is cooked, drain it, reserving some pasta water.
Add the pasta to the meat sauce, tossing gently to combine. Use the reserved pasta water to adjust the consistency of the sauce if necessary.

Molise

A tour of Molise, a region in southern Italy known for its untouched landscapes, ancient traditions, and archaeological sites, offers a journey through one of Italy's least explored areas. Here's what a tour through Molise might include:

Day 1: Arrival in Campobasso

Begin your journey in Campobasso, the capital of Molise. Explore the Castello Monforte and the Museo dei Misteri, dedicated to the town's annual religious procession. Stroll through the old town, enjoying its medieval atmosphere.

Day 2: The Samnite Heritage

Visit the Samnite Museum in Campobasso, showcasing the history of the ancient Samnite people of the region.

Travel to the archaeological site of Saepinum (Altilia), an ancient Samnite town later Romanized, featuring well-preserved ruins.

Day 3: Termoli and the Adriatic Coast

Head to Termoli, a charming coastal town with a picturesque historic center. Visit the Cathedral of Saint Basso and explore the ancient castle overlooking the sea. Enjoy a relaxing afternoon on the beaches of Termoli.

Day 4: Agnone and the Art of Bell Making

Visit Agnone, an ancient town known for its bell foundry, the Pontificia Fonderia Marinelli, one of the oldest in the world.

Explore the town's historic center and the International Bell Museum. Sample local cheeses, such as caciocavallo, in one of Agnone's traditional dairy shops.

Day 5: The Matese Mountains

Spend a day in the Matese mountain range, enjoying its stunning natural landscapes. Visit the Matese Regional Park for hiking or, in the winter, skiing. Explore the charming mountain villages, such as San Massimo and Campitello Matese.

Day 6: Ancient Traditions in Larino and Guardialfiera

Travel to Larino, known for its Roman amphitheater and the Cathedral of Saint Pardo. Visit Guardialfiera, particularly the ancient Church of Santa Maria di Canneto. In the evening, enjoy traditional Molisan cuisine, which blends Italian and Adriatic flavors.

Day 7: Departure

Return to Campobasso for any last-minute sightseeing or shopping. Depart from Campobasso's train station or the nearest airport.

This tour offers a comprehensive exploration of Molise, showcasing its rich history, cultural traditions, and natural beauty. Each day presents a new facet of this often overlooked but fascinating region of Italy.

Fusilli

Homemade pasta from Molise

Homemade pasta from Molise, a region in southern Italy, reflects the area's culinary traditions which blend elements of both its mountainous interior and Adriatic coastline. The pasta in Molise is known for its simplicity and the use of locally sourced ingredients.

Cavatelli: One of the most iconic pasta types from Molise. These are small, shell-shaped pasta made from durum wheat flour, water, and sometimes a little salt. Cavatelli are often served with a hearty meat sauce or a simpler tomato and basil sauce.

Fusilli Molisani: Also known as 'fusilli al ferretto,' these are long, twisted pasta shapes made by winding the dough around a knitting needle or a thin rod. They are typically paired with rich, meat based sauces.

Maccheroni alla Chitarra: While more associated with Abruzzo, neighboring Molise also enjoys this type of pasta. Made by pressing sheets of pasta dough through a tool called a 'chitarra' to create long, square-shaped spaghetti, it's typically served with a lamb or pork ragù.

Caserecce: This pasta is known for its distinctive, rustic appearance and its ability to hold onto sauces very well, making it a popular choice for a variety of Italian dishes.

Cavatelli al Sugo 'Vedovo' di Montenero
Cavatelli with 'Widowed' Sauce from Montenero

Ingredients

For the Cavatelli:
400 gr of semolina flour
200 ml of water (approximately)
A pinch of salt

For the Sugo 'Vedovo':
50 ml of olive oil
2 cloves of garlic, minced
400 gr of crushed tomatoes
A handful of fresh basil leaves
Salt and pepper (to taste)
Chili flakes (optional, to taste)

Instructions

Making the Cavatelli:
In a large bowl, combine the semolina flour and salt. Gradually add water, kneading until a smooth and firm dough forms. Let the dough rest, covered, for about 30 minutes. Take small pieces of dough and roll them into long "snakes". Cut into small pieces and use your fingers or a knife to drag each piece across the board, forming a curled shape with a hollow center. Boil the cavatelli in a large pot of salted water until they float to the surface and are al dente.

Preparing the Sugo 'Vedovo':
In a large pan, heat the olive oil. Add the minced garlic (and chili flakes if using) and cook until fragrant but not browned. Stir in the crushed tomatoes. Season with salt and pepper. Let the sauce simmer for about 20-30 minutes, allowing the flavors to meld together. Add the basil leaves in the last few minutes of cooking.

Once the cavatelli is cooked, drain it, reserving a bit of the pasta water. Add the cavatelli to the sauce, tossing gently. Use the reserved pasta water to adjust the sauce consistency if needed.

Caserecce alla Salsiccia e Cime di Rapa
Caserecce with Sausage and Broccoli Rabe

Ingredients

For the Caserecce:
400 gr of semolina flour
200 ml of water (approximately)
A pinch of salt

For the Sauce:
300 gr of Italian sausage (casing removed)
300 gr of cime di rapa (broccoli rabe), trimmed and chopped
50 ml of olive oil
3 cloves of garlic, minced
1 red chili pepper, chopped (or chili flakes to taste)
Salt and pepper (to taste)

Instructions

Making the Caserecce:
In a large bowl, mix the semolina flour and salt. Gradually add water, kneading until a firm, smooth dough forms. Let the dough rest, covered, for about 30 minutes.

Forming Caserecce:
Roll out the dough into thin ropes, then cut into small segments. Roll each segment against the surface or a fork to form the twisted caserecce shape.

Cook the caserecce in boiling salted water until al dente.

Preparing the Sauce:
In a large pan, cook the sausage over medium heat, breaking it into small pieces, until browned and cooked through. In another pan, heat olive oil. Add garlic and chili pepper, cooking until fragrant. Add the cime di rapa and sauté until tender. Mix the cooked sausage with the sautéed cime di rapa. Season with salt and pepper.

Once the caserecce is cooked, drain it, saving a bit of the pasta water. Add the caserecce to the pan with sausage and cime di rapa. Toss to combine, adding a little pasta water if needed to loosen the sauce.

Campania

A tour of Campania, a region in southwestern Italy known for its rich history, stunning coastline, and vibrant culture, offers an unforgettable experience.

Day 1: Arrival in Naples

Start your journey in Naples, the vibrant capital of Campania. Explore the historic center, a UNESCO World Heritage site, with its narrow streets, ancient churches, and famous pizzerias. Visit the Naples National Archaeological Museum, home to one of the world's finest collections of Greco-Roman artifacts.

Day 2: Pompeii and Mount Vesuvius

Take a day trip to Pompeii, the ancient city preserved by the eruption of Mount Vesuvius in 79 AD. Explore the ruins, including the Forum, the baths, and the villas with their preserved frescoes.

If time allows, hike up to the crater of Mount Vesuvius for panoramic views of the Bay of Naples.

Day 3: The Amalfi Coast

Drive along the Amalfi Coast, known for its dramatic cliffs and stunning sea views. Stop at Positano, a picturesque town with colorful houses cascading down to the sea. Visit Amalfi and its famous cathedral, and enjoy a traditional seafood lunch.

Day 4: The Island of Capri

Take a ferry to the island of Capri, a luxurious retreat famous for its natural beauty. Visit the Blue Grotto, a sea cave illuminated with blue light, and the Gardens of Augustus for breathtaking views.

Stroll through Capri town and enjoy shopping in its chic boutiques.

Day 5: Historical Caserta

Spend a day in Caserta, home to the Royal Palace of Caserta, often compared to Versailles for its grandeur. Explore the palace's opulent rooms and vast gardens. Visit the nearby ancient town of Caserta vecchia, with its medieval streets and Romanesque cathedral.

Day 6: Sorrento and Limoncello Tasting

Head to Sorrento, a charming town overlooking the Bay of Naples. Stroll through the historic center, visit the Cathedral of Sorrento, and relax in one of the many cafes.

Enjoy a Limoncello tasting session; this lemon liqueur is a specialty of the region.

Day 7: Departure

Spend your last day in Naples.

Enjoy some last-minute shopping, perhaps purchasing traditional crafts like hand-painted ceramics or Neapolitan music boxes.

Savor a final Neapolitan pizza before your departure.

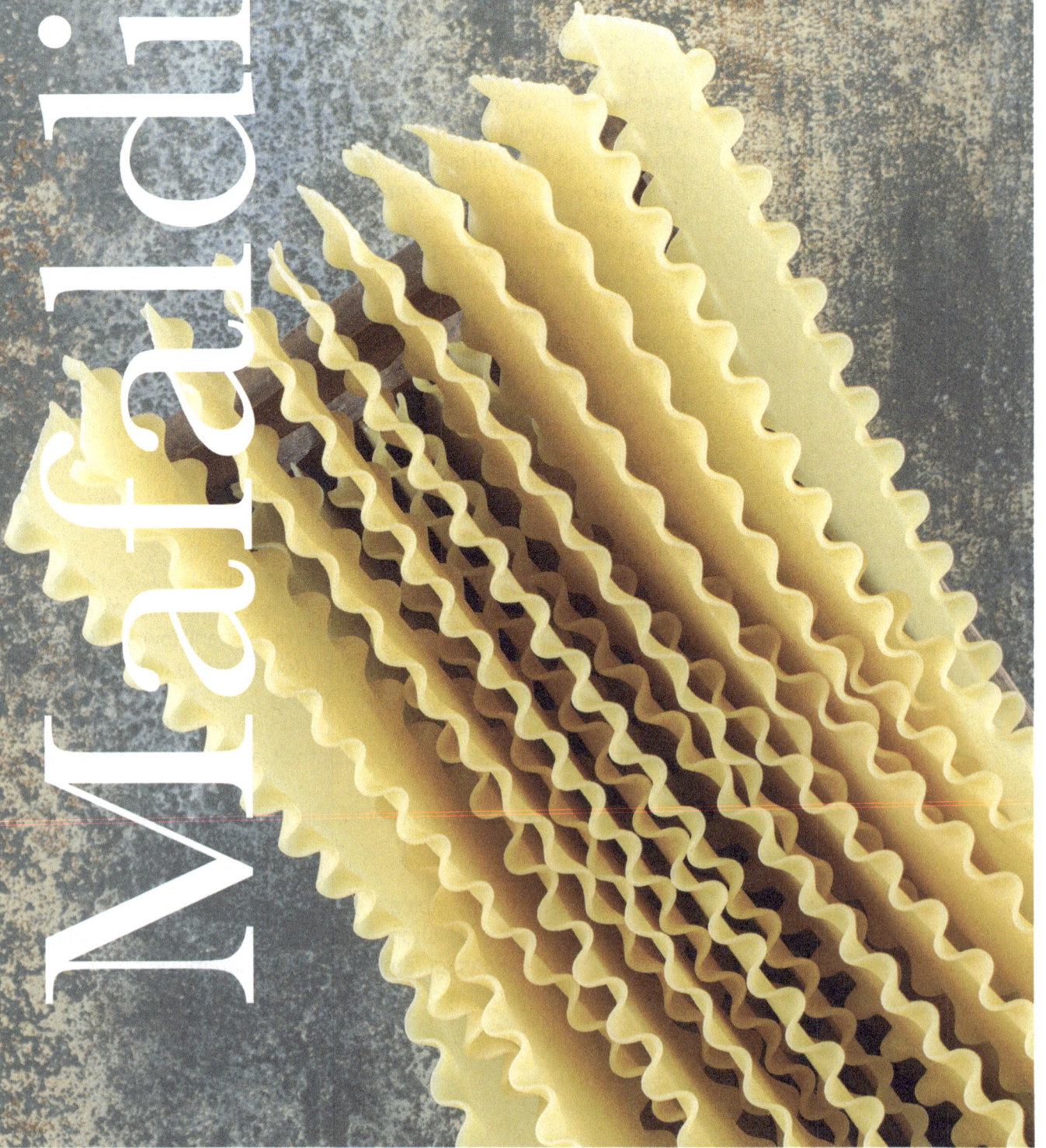

Mafaldine

Homemade pasta from Campania

Campania, a region in southwestern Italy renowned for its rich culinary history, is home to several types of unique and traditional homemade pasta. This region is famous for its contribution to Italian cuisine, especially pasta. Here are some of the typical, genuine kinds of homemade pasta you'll find in Campania.

Scialatielli: Originating from the Amalfi Coast, scialatielli is a fresh pasta similar to fettuccine but shorter and thicker. It's traditionally made with flour, water, salt, and sometimes milk, with herbs mixed into the dough. Scialatielli pairs well with seafood sauces.

Fusilli Napoletani: These are long, corkscrew-shaped pasta made by twisting spaghetti around a knitting needle. They are often served with ragù Napoletano, a slow-cooked meat sauce.

Lagane: This is an ancient type of pasta, similar to tagliatelle but wider. In Campania, it's often paired with chickpeas in a simple yet hearty dish.

Mafaldine: Also known as "reginette" (little queens), these are ribbon-shaped pasta with wavy edges on both sides, created in honor of Queen Mafalda of Savoy. They are typically served with rich, meaty sauces.

Paccheri: Large, tube-shaped pasta, paccheri is excellent for hearty sauces or in baked pasta dishes. They are often stuffed with cheese, meat, or vegetables.

Strascinati: These are hand-pulled and shaped pasta, similar to orecchiette but larger. Strascinati are often served with robust vegetable or meat sauces.

Pasta, Patate e Provola alla Napoletana
Pasta and Potatoes with Provola in the Neapolitan Style

Ingredients

For the Fresh Pasta:
300 gr of '00' flour
3 large eggs
A pinch of salt

For the Dish:
300 gr of yellow potatoes, peeled and diced
100 gr of smoked provola cheese, diced
50 ml of olive oil
1 onion, finely chopped
1 carrot, finely chopped
1 celery stalk, finely chopped
400 gr of crushed tomatoes
1000 ml of water or vegetable broth
Salt and pepper (to taste)
A handful of fresh parsley, chopped

Instructions

Making the Fresh Pasta:
In a large bowl, mix the '00' flour with a pinch of salt. Create a well in the center and crack the eggs into it. Gradually incorporate the flour into the eggs until a dough forms. Knead the dough on a floured surface until smooth and elastic, about 10 minutes. Cover the dough with a cloth and let it rest for 30 minutes. Roll out the dough into thin sheets, then cut it into your desired pasta shape, such as tagliatelle or fettuccine.

Preparing the Dish:
In a large pot, heat the olive oil. Add the chopped onion, carrot, and celery. Sauté until the onion is translucent. Add the diced potatoes and stir for a few minutes.
Add Tomatoes and Broth: Mix in the crushed tomatoes and add water or vegetable broth. Bring to a boil, then reduce to a simmer. Season with salt and pepper.
Let it cook until the potatoes start to become tender.
Cook Pasta: Add the fresh pasta to the pot. Cook until the pasta is al dente and the potatoes are fully tender.
The dish should be thick and stew-like. A few minutes before the dish is done, add the diced provola cheese, allowing it to melt into the dish. Stir in the chopped parsley.

Pasta Fagioli e Cozze
Pasta Beans and Mussels

Ingredients

For the Fresh Pasta:
300 gr of '00' flour
3 large eggs
A pinch of salt

For the Dish:
500 gr of mussels, cleaned and debearded
200 gr of cannellini beans
(soaked overnight and cooked, or canned)
50 ml of olive oil
2 cloves of garlic, minced
200 gr of crushed tomatoes
1 small onion, finely chopped
100 ml of white wine
Salt and pepper (to taste)
A handful of fresh parsley, chopped
500 ml of water or vegetable broth

Instructions

Making the Fresh Pasta:
In a large bowl, mix the flour and salt. Make a well in the center, add the eggs, and gradually incorporate the flour until a dough forms. Knead on a floured surface until smooth and elastic. Let the dough rest, covered, for about 30 minutes. Roll out the dough into thin sheets, then cut it into your desired pasta shape, like tagliatelle or fettuccine.

Preparing the Dish:
In a pan, heat a little olive oil. Add half the garlic and the mussels. Pour in the white wine and cover. Cook until the mussels open, then remove from heat. Discard any mussels that don't open. In a pot, heat the remaining olive oil. Add the onion and remaining garlic, sautéing until translucent. Add Tomatoes and Beans: Stir in the crushed tomatoes and cooked cannellini beans. Add water or broth as needed to achieve a slightly soupy consistency.
Add salt, pepper, and half of the chopped parsley.
Add the fresh pasta to the pot, cooking until al dente.
Combine with Mussels: Once the pasta is cooked, add the mussels (with their liquid) to the pot. Stir everything gently to combine, and let it simmer for a few more minutes.
Plate the Pasta Fagioli e Cozze, garnishing with the remaining fresh parsley.

Pasta Broccoli e Ceci
Pasta with Broccoli and Chickpeas

Ingredients

For the Fresh Pasta:
300 gr of '00' flour
3 large eggs
A pinch of salt

For the Dish:
300 gr of broccoli, cut into florets
200 gr of cooked chickpeas
(canned or soaked overnight and cooked)
50 ml of olive oil
2 cloves of garlic, minced
Chili flakes (to taste)
Salt and pepper (to taste)
100 ml of water or vegetable broth
Grated Parmesan cheese (optional, for serving)

Instructions

Making the Fresh Pasta:
Combine the flour and salt in a large bowl. Create a well in the center, add the eggs, and gradually mix the flour into the eggs until a dough forms. Knead on a floured surface until smooth and elastic. Let the dough rest, covered, for about 30 minutes. Roll out the dough into thin sheets, then cut into your desired pasta shape, such as tagliatelle or fettuccine.

Preparing the Dish:
In a large pot of boiling salted water, cook the broccoli florets until tender. Remove the broccoli and set aside, keeping the water boiling for cooking the pasta.
Sauté Garlic and Chickpeas: In a skillet, heat the olive oil. Add the garlic and chili flakes, cooking until fragrant. Add the chickpeas and sauté for a few minutes.
Add Broccoli: Add the cooked broccoli to the skillet. Season with salt and pepper. Cook the fresh pasta in the boiling water until al dente. Drain the pasta, reserving a cup of the pasta water. Add the pasta to the skillet with broccoli and chickpeas. Add water or broth as needed to keep the dish moist. Gently toss everything together, allowing the flavors to meld for a few minutes.
Plate the pasta broccoli e ceci, optionally topping with grated Parmesan cheese.

Gnocchi alla Sorrentina
Gnocchi Sorrento-Style

Ingredients

For the Gnocchi:
1000 gr. of potatoes
(preferably starchy varieties like Russets)
300 gr. of '00' flour (or all-purpose flour)
1 large egg
Salt (to taste)

For the Sauce:
400 gr. of crushed tomatoes
2 cloves of garlic, minced
30 ml of olive oil
Salt and pepper (to taste)
A handful of fresh basil leaves

For the Baking:
200 gr. of fresh mozzarella cheese, diced
50 gr. of grated Parmesan cheese

Instructions

Making the Gnocchi:

Boil the potatoes with their skins on until they are completely tender. Once cool enough to handle, peel the potatoes and mash them until smooth. On a floured surface, make a well in the center of the mashed potatoes. Add the flour, egg, and a pinch of salt. Gently combine to form a soft dough. Roll pieces of the dough into long "snakes", then cut into small pillow-shaped pieces. Press each piece against a fork or a gnocchi board to create ridges. Boil the gnocchi in salted water until they float to the top.

In a saucepan, heat the olive oil. Add the minced garlic and cook until fragrant. Stir in the crushed tomatoes. Season with salt and pepper. Let the sauce simmer for about 20 minutes. Add the basil leaves towards the end.

Preheat your oven to 190°C (375°F).

After cooking the gnocchi, combine them with the tomato sauce in a baking dish. Scatter the diced mozzarella and grated Parmesan over the top.

Bake in the oven until the cheese is melted and bubbly, about 20-25 minutes. Enjoy your homemade Gnocchi alla Sorrentina hot from the oven, with its comforting blend of soft gnocchi, rich tomato sauce, and melted cheese.

Apulia

A tour of Puglia (Apulia), a region in southeastern Italy known for its whitewashed hill towns, centuries-old farmland, and lengthy Mediterranean coastline, offers a blend of cultural, historical, and natural experiences.

Day 1: Arrival in Bari

Begin your journey in Bari, the capital of the Puglia region.

Explore the old town of Bari Vecchia, visiting the Basilica di San Nicola and Bari Cathedral. Stroll along the seafront promenade and enjoy a traditional dinner in the city, perhaps trying the local "orecchiette" pasta.

Day 2: Trulli of Alberobello and Ostuni

Visit Alberobello, famous for its unique trulli buildings, white conical roofed houses that are a UNESCO World Heritage site.

In the afternoon, travel to Ostuni, known as the "White City" for its whitewashed walls and houses. Enjoy the panoramic views of the surrounding olive groves and the Adriatic Sea from Ostuni.

Day 3: Lecce, the Florence of the South

Head to Lecce, renowned for its baroque architecture, including the Basilica di Santa Croce and the Lecce Cathedral. Walk through the charming streets and visit artisanal shops selling local crafts, such as papier-mâché items. Try some of Lecce's traditional dishes, like "rustico leccese" or "pasticciotto".

Day 4: The Itria Valley

Explore the Itria Valley, known for its olive trees, vineyards, and charming towns. Visit towns like Martina Franca, with its baroque buildings, and Locorotondo, known for its circular structure and white alleys. Sample local wines, such as Primitivo or Negroamaro, in one of the valley's many wineries.

Day 5: Gargano Peninsula and Vieste

Travel to the Gargano Peninsula, a mountainous area with beautiful coastlines. Visit Vieste, a seaside town with stunning beaches and a picturesque old town. Explore the Umbra Forest in the Gargano National Park or take a boat trip to the sea caves along the coast.

Day 6: Matera in Basilicata

Although in the neighboring region of Basilicata, a visit to Matera, famous for its ancient cave dwellings called "sassi," is highly recommended. Explore these unique cave houses, churches, and monasteries, and learn about Matera's fascinating history. Return to Puglia in the evening.

Day 7: Departure from Bari

Spend your last day in Bari, enjoying the city's vibrant street life and perhaps doing some last-minute shopping for local products like olive oil, taralli, and wine. Depart from Bari's international airport or train station.

Orecchiette

Homemade pasta from Puglia

Homemade pasta from Puglia, a region in southeastern Italy, is known for its simplicity and the use of high-quality, local ingredients. Puglian pasta is a cornerstone of the region's culinary tradition, showcasing the area's agricultural richness.

Orecchiette: Perhaps the most iconic pasta from Puglia, orecchiette translates to "little ears," reflecting their shape. They are made with just durum wheat semolina flour and water. Traditionally, orecchiette is served with "cime di rapa" (broccoli rabe) or a rich tomato sauce.

Cavatelli: Similar to orecchiette but elongated, cavatelli are also made with durum wheat and water. They have a rolled edge that's perfect for catching thicker sauces or for being served with vegetables and legumes.

Troccoli: These are thick, square-cut spaghetti, typically made with a blend of semolina and all-purpose flour. In Puglia, troccoli might be served with a hearty tomato and meat sauce.

Sagne 'ncannulate: Long, twisted pasta ribbons, often served with a rich tomato sauce, sometimes with the addition of ricotta or pecorino cheese.

Minchiareddhi, also known as 'Capunti': A small, elongated pasta that is indented in the middle, resembling an open pea pod. They are often served with vegetable based sauces.

Orecchiette alle Cime di Rapa con Briciole di Tarallo
Orecchiette with Broccoli Rabe and Tarallo Crumbs

Ingredients

For the Orecchiette:
400 gr. of semolina flour
200 ml of water (approximately)
A pinch of salt

For the Dish:
500 gr. of cime di rapa (broccoli rabe), trimmed and chopped
50 ml of olive oil
2 cloves of garlic, minced
1 anchovy fillet (optional)
Red chili flakes (to taste)
Salt and pepper (to taste)

For the Tarallo Crumbs:
100 gr of taralli (traditional Italian crackers), crushed into crumbs

Instructions

Making the Orecchiette:

In a bowl, mix the semolina flour and salt. Gradually add water, kneading until a firm dough forms.

Rest the Dough: Let the dough rest for about 30 minutes. Forming Orecchiette: Take small pieces of dough and shape them into small discs. Then, using your thumb, press and drag each disc to turn it inside out, forming the classic orecchiette shape. Cook the orecchiette in boiling salted water until they float to the surface and are al dente.

In a large pan, cook the cime di rapa in boiling water for a few minutes until tender. Drain and set aside.

In the same pan, heat olive oil over medium heat.

Add garlic, anchovy (if using), and chili flakes. Cook until the garlic is golden and the anchovy dissolves.

Combine with Cime di Rapa: Add the cooked cime di rapa to the pan. Season with salt and pepper and sauté for a few minutes.

Drain the cooked orecchiette and add them to the pan with the cime di rapa. Toss everything together to coat the pasta evenly. Sprinkle the crushed taralli over the pasta. Plate the orecchiette alle cime di rapa con briciole di tarallo and serve hot.

Cavatelli Cozze e Ceci
Cavatelli with Mussels and Chickpeas

Ingredients

For the Cavatelli:
400 gr of semolina flour
200 ml of water (approximately)
A pinch of salt

For the Dish:
500 gr of mussels, cleaned and debearded
200 gr of cooked chickpeas
(canned or soaked overnight and cooked)
50 ml of olive oil
2 cloves of garlic, minced
1 small onion, finely chopped
150 ml of white wine
400 gr of crushed tomatoes
Salt and pepper (to taste)
A handful of fresh parsley, chopped

Instructions

Making the Cavatelli:
In a large bowl, mix the semolina flour and salt.
Gradually add water, kneading until a firm dough forms.
Let the dough rest, covered, for about 30 minutes.

Forming Cavatelli
Roll small pieces of dough into long "snakes", then cut into small pillow-shaped pieces. Press each piece against a surface with two fingers to create the classic cavatelli shape. Cook the cavatelli in boiling salted water until they float to the surface and are al dente.

In a pan, heat some olive oil over medium heat. Add half the garlic and the mussels. Pour in the white wine and cover. Cook until the mussels open, then remove from heat. Discard any mussels that don't open.

In a pot, heat the remaining olive oil. Add the onion and remaining garlic, cooking until the onion is translucent. Stir in the crushed tomatoes and cooked chickpeas.

Season with salt and pepper. Once the mussels are cooked, add them to the pot with their liquid. Let everything simmer together for about 10-15 minutes.

Once the cavatelli are cooked, drain them, reserving some pasta water. Add the cavatelli to the pot with the mussels and chickpeas. Toss to combine, adding reserved pasta water if needed. Garnish the Cavatelli Cozze e Ceci alla Pugliese with fresh parsley and serve hot.

Troccoli del Gargano alla Crema di Cime di Rapa, Polvere di Crusco e Alici

Troccoli from Gargano with Broccoli Rabe Cream, Crusco Pepper Powder and Anchovies

Ingredients

For the Troccoli:
400 gr of semolina flour
200 ml of water (approximately)
A pinch of salt

For the Cream of Broccoli Rabe (Cime di Rapa):
500 gr of cime di rapa (broccoli rabe), trimmed and chopped
30 ml of olive oil
2 cloves of garlic, minced
Salt and pepper (to taste)

For the Crusco Pepper Powder:
2-3 dried Crusco peppers (or substitute with mild dried red chili peppers), crushed into powder

Additional Ingredients:
4-5 anchovy fillets
Extra virgin olive oil for finishing
Grated Pecorino cheese (optional)

Instructions

Making the Troccoli:
Mix the semolina flour and salt in a large bowl.
Gradually add water, kneading until a firm dough forms.
Let it rest for about 30 minutes.

Forming Troccoli:
Roll out the dough and cut it into thick, square-cut strips using a knife or a troccoli cutter. Cook the troccoli in boiling salted water until al dente.

Preparing the Cream of Broccoli Rabe:
Boil the cime di rapa until tender. Drain and reserve some cooking water. In a pan, heat the olive oil and sauté the garlic. Transfer the cime di rapa to a blender, adding garlic and a bit of the cooking water. Blend until smooth. Season with salt and pepper.

Drain the troccoli, reserving some pasta water. Toss the troccoli with the broccoli rabe cream, adding pasta water if necessary to achieve a creamy consistency.

In a separate pan, gently heat the anchovy fillets in a bit of olive oil until they dissolve into a paste. Mix this into the pasta. Sprinkle the Crusco pepper powder over the pasta. Plate the Troccoli del Gargano, drizzling with extra virgin olive oil and optionally topping with grated Pecorino.

Basilicata

A tour of Basilicata, a hidden gem in Southern Italy, offers a journey through unique landscapes, ancient history, and rich cultural traditions.

Day 1: Arrival in Potenza

Begin your tour in Potenza, the regional capital of Basilicata.

Explore the city's historic center, visiting the Romanesque Cathedral and the National Archaeological Museum.

Enjoy dinner at a local trattoria, sampling Basilicata's rustic cuisine.

Day 2: The Dolomiti Lucane and Pietrapertosa

Head to the Dolomiti Lucane, a stunning mountain range known for its unique rock formations. Explore Pietrapertosa, one of Italy's highest-altitude villages, with its ancient Saracen castle.

For adventure seekers, try the "Volo dell'Angelo" (Flight of the Angel) zip-line between Pietrapertosa and Castelmezzano.

Day 3: Matera - The City of Stones

Visit Matera, known for its historic "Sassi" cave dwellings, a UNESCO World Heritage Site. Explore the ancient cave churches, the Cathedral, and the MUSMA (Museum of Contemporary Sculpture).

In the evening, enjoy a walk through the illuminated Sassi, followed by dinner in a cave restaurant.

Day 4: The Ionian Coast and Metaponto

Travel to the Ionian Coast, known for its beautiful beaches and ancient Greek ruins.

Visit Metaponto, where you can explore the archaeological park and museum, featuring remains of Greek temples and an ancient agora.

Day 5: Pollino National Park

Spend a day in Pollino National Park, the largest national park in Italy. Enjoy hiking or horseback riding, exploring the park's diverse flora and fauna. Visit an agriturismo for a lunch made with local, organic products.

Day 6: The Ghost Town of Craco

Explore Craco, an eerie yet fascinating abandoned medieval town. Learn about the town's history and the reasons behind its evacuation. Enjoy panoramic views of the surrounding valleys.

Day 7: Lucanian Wine and Farewell

Visit a local vineyard in the Aglianico del Vulture wine region.

Enjoy a wine tasting session, learning about this robust red wine made from the Aglianico grape. Spend your final evening in Potenza or Matera, reflecting on your journey through Basilicata.

Depart from Potenza or Matera, carrying with you memories of a region filled with natural beauty, ancient history, and a deep sense of tradition.

Treccce

Homemade pasta from Basilicata

Homemade pasta from Basilicata, a region in Southern Italy, is deeply rooted in the area's culinary traditions and reflects the region's agricultural heritage and rustic flavors.

Strascinati and Orecchiette: One of the most distinctive types of pasta from Basilicata is "strascinati," which are hand-formed and resemble small, concave disks with ridges on one side. These are similar to "orecchiette" (little ears), commonly found in neighboring Puglia, but strascinati are typically larger and have a rougher texture, making them ideal for holding hearty sauces.

Fusilli: Another typical pasta from Basilicata is handmade fusilli. Unlike the machine-extruded fusilli familiar to many, these are hand-rolled and twisted, often using a knitting needle or a similar tool. This process gives them a unique helical shape and a texture that excellently absorbs sauces.

Trecce and Lagane: "Trecce," meaning braids, are a type of pasta often made in the region. "Lagane," a wide and flat pasta, is another traditional shape, similar to tagliatelle but somewhat wider.

Fusilli al Ferretto con Peperoni Cruschi
Fusilli on a Wire with Crispy Sweet Peppers

Ingredients
For the Fusilli:
400 gr of semolina flour
200 ml of water (approximately)
A pinch of salt
For the Peperoni Cruschi:
4-5 dried sweet red peppers (Peperoni Cruschi)
Olive oil (for frying)

Instructions
Making the Fusilli:
In a large bowl, mix the semolina flour and salt. Gradually add water, kneading until a firm, smooth dough forms. Let it rest, covered, for about 30 minutes.
Forming Fusilli:
Take small pieces of dough and roll them into long, thin ropes. Wrap each rope around a ferretto (a traditional iron rod) or a wooden skewer, then roll back and forth to create the spiral shape of fusilli. Slide the pasta off the rod. Boil the fusilli in salted water until they are al dente.
Preparing the Peperoni Cruschi:
Remove stems and seeds from the dried peppers.
Cut them into large pieces. Heat a generous amount of olive oil in a pan. Fry the pepper pieces briefly until they become crisp but not burnt. This should only take a few seconds. Remove and drain on paper towels.
Once the fusilli is cooked, drain it, reserving a bit of the pasta water. Place the fusilli back in the pot or a serving bowl. Crumble the fried peperoni cruschi over the pasta. Toss: Gently toss the fusilli with the pepper, adding a bit of pasta water if needed to moisten. Plate the Fusilli al Ferretto con Peperoni Cruschi, enjoying the unique texture and flavor of the crispy peppers with the fresh pasta.

Lagane e Ceci
Lagane and Chickpeas

Ingredients

For the Lagane:
400 gr of semolina flour
200 ml of water (approximately)
A pinch of salt

For the Ceci (Chickpeas):
300 gr of dried chickpeas (soaked overnight)
Water (for soaking and cooking)

For the Sauce:
50 ml of olive oil
1 onion, finely chopped
2 cloves of garlic, minced
A sprig of rosemary
Salt and pepper (to taste)
400 gr of crushed tomatoes

Instructions

Preparing the Chickpeas:
Soak the dried chickpeas overnight in plenty of water.
Cook Chickpeas: Drain and cook the chickpeas in fresh water until tender, about 1-2 hours. Reserve the cooking water.

Making the Lagane:
In a large bowl, mix the semolina flour and salt. Gradually add water, kneading until a firm dough forms.
Rest the Dough: Let it rest for about 30 minutes.

Forming Lagane:
Roll out the dough thinly. Cut it into wide, short strips (similar to tagliatelle but wider and shorter).
Cook the lagane in boiling salted water until al dente.

Preparing the Sauce:
In a large pan, heat olive oil. Add the onion, garlic, and rosemary, cooking until the onion is soft. Stir in the crushed tomatoes. Season with salt and pepper. Let the sauce simmer for about 15-20 minutes. Drain the lagane, reserving some pasta water. Add the lagane to the sauce along with the cooked chickpeas. If needed, add some of the chickpea cooking water to achieve the desired consistency. Let everything cook together for a few more minutes to meld the flavors. Plate the Lagane e Ceci, offering a hearty and comforting meal with a rich blend of pasta and chickpeas.

Orecchiette, Erbette di Campo e Mollica

Orecchiette with Wild Greens and Breadcrumbs

Ingredients

For the Orecchiette:
400 gr of semolina flour
200 ml of water (approximately)
A pinch of salt
For the Dish:
500 gr of mixed wild greens
(such as dandelion, chicory, or spinach)
4-5 dried sweet red peppers (Peperoni Cruschi)
50 ml of olive oil
2 cloves of garlic, minced
100 gr of breadcrumbs
Salt and pepper (to taste)

Instructions

Making the Orecchiette:
In a large bowl, mix the semolina flour and salt. Gradually add water, kneading until a firm, smooth dough forms. Let it rest for about 30 minutes.
Forming Orecchiette:
Take small pieces of dough and roll them into balls.
Then, using your thumb, press and drag each ball to form the classic orecchiette shape. Cook the orecchiette in boiling salted water until they float to the surface and are al dente. Wash the wild greens thoroughly. Blanch them in boiling water, then drain and set aside.
Clean the dried peppers by removing stems and seeds. Fry them briefly in hot olive oil until they become crispy but not burnt. Remove and let cool, then crush into small pieces. Prepare Mollica (Breadcrumbs): In the same oil, fry the minced garlic until golden. Add breadcrumbs and toast until golden and crispy.
In another pan, heat a bit of olive oil. Add the blanched greens and sauté for a few minutes. Season with salt and pepper. Drain the cooked orecchiette and add them to the pan with the greens. Toss to combine. Sprinkle the crushed Cruschi peppers and garlic breadcrumbs over the pasta.
Plate the Orecchiette con Erbette di Campo, Cruschi e Mollica, offering a beautiful blend of textures and flavors, with the earthiness of the greens complemented by the crunchiness of the peppers and breadcrumbs.

Calabria

A tour of Calabria, located in the southern part of Italy and known for its rich history, stunning coastline, and unique cultural heritage, is an unforgettable experience. Here's a description of what a tour through Calabria might include:

Day 1: Arrival in Reggio Calabria

Begin your journey in Reggio Calabria, the biggest city of the region. Visit the National Archaeological Museum, famous for the Riace Bronzes, two remarkable Greek bronze statues. Stroll along the Lungomare Falcomatà, one of the most beautiful seafront promenades in Italy.

Day 2: The Aspromonte National Park

Explore the Aspromonte National Park, known for its rich biodiversity and breathtaking landscapes. Enjoy hiking trails with views of the Tyrrhenian and Ionian seas. Discover remote villages and ancient ruins within the park.

Day 3: Scilla and Chianalea

Visit the charming fishing village of Scilla, with its legendary seafront and Castle of Ruffo. Explore Chianalea, a picturesque district right on the water, often referred to as the "Venice of the South." Enjoy a seafood dinner in a local trattoria, tasting dishes made with the freshest catch.

Day 4: The Sila Plateau

Head to the Sila Plateau, an area with dense forests, clear lakes, and pure air. Enjoy outdoor activities like hiking, mountain biking, or boating on the Sila's lakes. Visit traditional villages and taste local products, such as Sila's renowned mushrooms and cheeses.

Day 5: Crotone and Capo Colonna

Travel to Crotone, an ancient city with Greek and Roman roots.
Visit the archaeological site of Capo Colonna, home to the remains of the Temple of Hera Lacinia. Enjoy the beautiful beaches around Capo Colonna.

Day 6: Tropea and the Tyrrhenian Coast

Visit Tropea, a picturesque town perched on cliffs overlooking the Tyrrhenian Sea. Explore the historic town center, with its narrow streets and impressive cathedral.
Relax on one of Tropea's stunning beaches, famous for their white sands and clear blue waters.

Day 7: Departure

Spend your last day enjoying the vibrant city life in Reggio Calabria. Visit local markets and shops for last-minute souvenirs, such as Calabrian chili products, bergamot perfumes, or handcrafted pottery.
Depart from Reggio Calabria or the nearest airport.

Fileja

Homemade pasta from Calabria

Homemade pasta from Calabria, a region in Southern Italy, is characterized by its rustic simplicity and the use of local ingredients. The pasta reflects the diverse culinary influences of the region, from its mountainous interior to its extensive coastline. Here are some key aspects of Calabrian homemade pasta:

Fileja or Filindeu: One of the most distinctive types of pasta from Calabria is "Fileja" (also known as "Filindeu" or "Maccheroncini"). This pasta is hand-rolled and shaped into long, thin spirals or twists. It's often served with hearty meat sauces or in broths.

Lagane: This is a wide, flat pasta, similar to tagliatelle but shorter in length. It's often served with chickpeas in a dish known as "Lagane e ceci."

Fusilli Calabresi: Handmade fusilli from Calabria are long, twisted pasta shapes made by wrapping the dough around a knitting needle or a thin rod. They are typically served with rich, spicy sauces.

Fileja con Salsa di Pomodoro e 'nduja
Fileja with Tomato Sauce and 'Nduja

Ingredients

For the Fileja:
400 gr of semolina flour
200 ml of water (approximately)
A pinch of salt
For the Tomato and 'Nduja Sauce:
50 gr of 'Nduja
400 gr of crushed tomatoes
30 ml of olive oil
1 onion, finely chopped
2 cloves of garlic, minced
Salt and pepper (to taste)
A handful of fresh basil leaves

Instructions

Making the Fileja:
In a large bowl, mix the semolina flour and salt.
Gradually add water, kneading until a firm dough forms.
Let the dough rest, covered, for about 30 minutes.
Forming Fileja:
Roll small pieces of dough into long, thin ropes. Then wrap each rope around a wooden stick (like a skewer) and roll back and forth to create the spiral shape. Slide off the stick.
Cook the fileja in boiling salted water until they float to the surface and are al dente.
Preparing the Sauce:
In a large pan, heat the olive oil. Add the onion and garlic, cooking until soft and translucent. Stir in the 'Nduja, breaking it up with a spoon. Cook until it's melted into the oil. Add the crushed tomatoes. Season with salt and pepper. Let the sauce simmer for about 15-20 minutes. Add the basil leaves towards the end. Once the fileja is cooked, drain it, reserving some pasta water.
Add the fileja to the tomato and 'Nduja sauce, tossing gently. Add reserved pasta water if needed to loosen the sauce. Plate the Fileja con Salsa di Pomodoro e 'Nduja, garnishing with additional basil leaves if desired.

Fileja alla Tropeana
Fileja Tropea-Style

Ingredients
For the Fileja:
400 gr of semolina flour
200 ml of water (approximately)
A pinch of salt
For the Sauce:
200 gr of red Tropea onions, thinly sliced
2 medium zucchini, sliced into thin rounds
400 gr of crushed tomatoes
30 ml of olive oil
2 cloves of garlic, minced
Salt and pepper (to taste)
A handful of fresh basil leaves
Chili flakes (optional, to taste)

Instructions
Making the Fileja:
In a large bowl, combine the semolina flour and salt.
Gradually add water, kneading until a firm dough forms.
Rest the Dough: Let the dough rest for about 30 minutes.
Forming Fileja:
Take small pieces of dough and roll them into long, thin ropes. Wrap each rope around a wooden stick (like a skewer) and roll back and forth to create the spiral shape. Slide off the stick. Cook the fileja in boiling salted water until they float to the surface and are al dente.
Preparing the Sauce:
In a large pan, heat the olive oil. Add the sliced Tropea onions and garlic. Cook until the onions are soft and translucent. Add the sliced zucchini to the pan and sauté until tender. Stir in the crushed tomatoes. Season with salt, pepper, and chili flakes if using. Let the sauce simmer for about 15-20 minutes, allowing the flavors to meld. Add the basil leaves towards the end. Once the fileja is cooked, drain it, reserving some pasta water. Add the fileja to the sauce, tossing to combine. Use the reserved pasta water to adjust the sauce's consistency if necessary.
Plate the Fileja alla Tropeana con Zucchine, garnishing with additional basil leaves or grated cheese if desired.

Lagane e Ceci alla Calabrese
Lagane and Chickpeas Calabrian Style

Ingredients

For the Lagane:
400 gr of all-purpose flour
200 ml of water (approximately)
A pinch of salt

For the Ceci (Chickpeas):
250 gr of dried chickpeas (soaked overnight)
Water (for soaking and cooking)

For the Sauce:
50 ml of olive oil
1 onion, finely chopped
2 cloves of garlic, minced
1 small red chili pepper, finely chopped (optional for heat)
Salt and pepper (to taste)
400 gr of crushed tomatoes
A sprig of rosemary

Instructions

Preparing the Chickpeas:
Soak the chickpeas overnight in plenty of water.

Cook Chickpeas:
Drain and cook the chickpeas in fresh water until tender, about 1-2 hours. Reserve the cooking water.

Making the Lagane:
Mix the flour and salt in a large bowl.
Gradually add water, kneading until a firm dough forms.
Rest the Dough: Let the dough rest for about 30 minutes.

Forming Lagane:
Roll out the dough thinly. Cut it into wide, short strips (similar to fettuccine but wider). Cook the lagane in boiling salted water until al dente.

Preparing the Sauce:
In a large pan, heat olive oil. Add the onion, garlic, and chili pepper. Cook until the onion is soft.
Stir in the crushed tomatoes and rosemary. Season with salt and pepper. Let the sauce simmer for about 15-20 minutes. Combine Pasta and Chickpeas: Drain the lagane, reserving some pasta water. Add the lagane to the sauce along with the cooked chickpeas. Add reserved pasta water or chickpea cooking water to achieve the desired consistency. Let everything cook together for a few more minutes to meld the flavors.
Plate the Lagane e Ceci alla Calabrese, garnishing with fresh herbs or grated cheese if desired.

Sardinia

A tour of Sardegna (Sardinia), an Italian island in the Mediterranean Sea known for its stunning beaches, ancient history, and unique cultural traditions, offers a diverse and enriching experience.

Day 1: Arrival in Cagliari

Begin your journey in Cagliari, the capital of Sardinia.

Explore the historic Castello district, visiting the Cagliari Cathedral and the Bastione di Saint Remy for panoramic city views.

Stroll along Poetto Beach and enjoy a seafood dinner at the marina.

Day 2: The South – Nora and Chia

Visit the archaeological site of Nora, an ancient Phoenician city, and explore its Roman ruins. Head to the beautiful beaches of Chia, known for their clear waters and soft sand.

Enjoy water sports or relax on the beach, and in the evening, sample local Sardinian cuisine.

Day 3: Barumini and the Sardinian Countryside

Travel to Barumini to visit the UNESCO World Heritage site of Su Nuraxi, an ancient nuragic complex.

Explore the Sardinian countryside, perhaps visiting a vineyard or an agriturismo for a taste of rural life and local products.

In the evening, return to Cagliari.

Day 4: The West Coast – Bosa and Alghero

Drive to Bosa, a picturesque town on the Temo River, known for its colorful houses and medieval castle.

Continue to Alghero, a Catalan-influenced town on the northwest coast, with beautiful beaches and a charming old town.

Explore the Neptune's Grotto, a stunning marine cave.

Day 5: The North – Costa Smeralda and La Maddalena Archipelago

Visit the Costa Smeralda, famous for its emerald waters and luxury resorts. Take a boat tour to the La Maddalena Archipelago, enjoying the pristine beaches and clear waters. Explore the main island of La Maddalena and its charming town.

Day 6: The East – Nuoro and the Gennargentu Mountains

Head to Nuoro, a cultural hub surrounded by mountains, and visit the Museo Etnografico Sardo to learn about Sardinian traditions.

Explore the Gennargentu National Park, offering hiking opportunities and stunning landscapes. Visit traditional mountain villages, such as Orgosolo, known for its murals.

Day 7: Departure from Olbia or Cagliari

Spend your last day in either Olbia or Cagliari, depending on your flight or ferry. Enjoy last-minute shopping for Sardinian crafts, such as ceramics or textiles. Depart from Olbia Costa Smeralda Airport or Cagliari Elmas Airport.

Culurgiones

Homemade pasta from Sardegna

Homemade pasta from Sardegna (Sardinia), an island with a rich culinary tradition, reflects the region's unique cultural influences and local ingredients. Sardinian pasta is known for its distinctive shapes and flavors.

Malloreddus (Gnocchetti Sardi): Perhaps the most iconic Sardinian pasta, malloreddus are small, ridged, shell-shaped pasta made from semolina flour and water, often flavored with saffron. They are typically served with a hearty meat sauce, often a sausage or lamb ragù, and topped with pecorino cheese.

Fregola (Fregula): Similar to couscous, fregola consists of small, toasted semolina balls. It's often cooked like risotto (fregola risottata) and is typically served with seafood and a saffron-infused broth, reflecting the island's coastal influences.

Culurgiones: These are Sardinian stuffed pasta, resembling large, ridged ravioli, typically filled with a mixture of potatoes, mint, and pecorino cheese. They are often served with a tomato sauce or simply dressed with melted butter and sage.

Lorighittas: A very unique and traditional pasta, lorighittas are ring-shaped and braided by hand, a technique that requires skill and patience. They are usually served with a tomato or meat-based sauce and are typical of the town of Morgongiori.

Fregula, Cozze e Pecorino
Fregula, Mussels, and Pecorino

Ingredients

For the Fregula:
200 gr. of semolina flour
100 ml of water (approximately)

For the Dish:
500 gr of mussels, cleaned and debearded
50 ml of olive oil
2 cloves of garlic, minced
1 small onion, finely chopped
200 ml of white wine
400 gr of cherry tomatoes, halved
Salt and pepper (to taste)
A handful of fresh parsley, chopped
50 gr of grated Pecorino cheese

Instructions

Making the Fregula:
In a bowl, mix the semolina flour with water, kneading until a firm but pliable dough forms.

Forming Fregula:
Rub small amounts of the dough between your palms to form tiny pellets, about the size of couscous or small peas. Let them dry on a baking sheet. Cook the fregula in boiling salted water until al dente, about 10 minutes.

Preparing the Dish:
In a large pan, heat some olive oil. Add half the garlic and the mussels. Pour in half of the white wine and cover. Cook until the mussels open, then remove from heat. Discard any mussels that don't open.

In another pot, heat the remaining olive oil. Add the onion and remaining garlic, cooking until translucent.

Add the cherry tomatoes and the rest of the wine. Cook until the tomatoes start to break down. Add salt, pepper, and most of the chopped parsley. Simmer for a few minutes.

Combine with Mussels: Add the cooked mussels to the tomato sauce. Once the fregula is cooked, drain and add it to the pan with the mussels and tomato sauce.

Gently mix the fregula with the sauce, allowing it to absorb the flavors. Plate the Fregula Cozze e Pecorino, sprinkling with grated Pecorino cheese and the remaining parsley.

Culurgiones in Salsa di Pomodoro
Culurgiones with Tomato Sauce

Ingredients

For the Culurgiones:
500 gr of '00' flour
250 ml of water (approximately)
A pinch of salt

For the Filling:
500 gr of potatoes, peeled and boiled
200 gr of Pecorino cheese, grated
A handful of fresh mint leaves, chopped
Salt and pepper (to taste)

For the Tomato Sauce:
400 gr of crushed tomatoes
30 ml of olive oil
1 onion, finely chopped
2 cloves of garlic, minced
Salt and pepper (to taste)
A handful of fresh basil leaves

Instructions

Making the Culurgiones:
Mix the flour and salt in a large bowl. Gradually add water, kneading until a smooth dough forms.
Let the dough rest, covered, for about 30 minutes.

Prepare Filling:
Mash the boiled potatoes and mix with grated Pecorino, chopped mint, salt, and pepper.

Forming Culurgiones:
Roll out the dough thinly. Cut into circles. Place a spoonful of filling in the center of each circle. Fold the dough over the filling and seal, pinching the edges to create a decorative pattern. Cook the culurgiones in boiling salted water until they float to the surface.

Preparing the Tomato Sauce:
In a pan, heat olive oil. Add the onion and garlic, cooking until soft. Stir in the crushed tomatoes. Season with salt and pepper. Let the sauce simmer for about 20 minutes. Add the basil leaves towards the end.

Once the culurgiones are cooked, drain them, reserving some pasta water. Add the culurgiones to the tomato sauce, tossing gently. Use reserved pasta water to adjust the sauce consistency if needed.

Lorighittas con Pesto di Ortica
Lorighittas with Nettle Sauce

Ingredients

For the Lorighittas:
400 gr of '00' flour (or all-purpose flour)
200 ml of water (approximately)
A pinch of salt

For the Nettle Pesto:
200 gr of fresh nettles (stinging nettles), blanched and chopped
2 cloves of garlic
50 gr of pine nuts or walnuts
50 gr of grated Pecorino cheese
100 ml of olive oil
Salt and pepper (to taste)
200 gr of fresh ricotta cheese

Instructions

Making the Lorighittas:
In a large bowl, combine the flour and salt. Gradually add water, kneading until a smooth and elastic dough forms. Let the dough rest, covered, for about 30 minutes.

Forming Lorighittas: Roll small pieces of dough into thin ropes. Form each rope into a ring and twist to create the characteristic double loop of lorighittas.

Press to seal the ends. Cook the lorighittas in boiling salted water until they float to the surface and are al dente.

Preparing the Nettle Pesto:
Wear gloves to handle fresh nettles. Blanch them in boiling water for a few minutes to remove the sting, then drain and chop.

Make Pesto: In a food processor, combine the blanched nettles, garlic, nuts, Pecorino cheese, olive oil, salt, and pepper. Blend until smooth.

Once the lorighittas are cooked, drain them, reserving a bit of the pasta water. Toss the lorighittas with the nettle pesto, adding reserved pasta water if needed to loosen the pesto. Serve the pasta with dollops of fresh ricotta on top.

Sicily

A tour of Sicily, the largest island in the Mediterranean Sea, known for its rich history, diverse landscapes, and vibrant culinary scene, offers a journey through ancient civilizations, stunning natural beauty, and a unique cultural heritage. Here's a description of what a tour through Sicily might include:

Day 1: Arrival in Palermo

Begin your journey in Palermo, the capital of Sicily.

Explore the historic city center, visiting landmarks like the Palermo Cathedral, the Norman Palace, and the Palatine Chapel.

Stroll through the bustling markets like Mercato di Ballarò or Vucciria and enjoy a traditional Sicilian dinner.

Day 2: Monreale and Cefalù

Visit the Cathedral of Monreale, known for its stunning golden mosaics. Travel to Cefalù, a charming coastal town with a beautiful Norman cathedral and lovely beach. Spend the afternoon relaxing by the sea or exploring the medieval streets.

Day 3: The Valley of the Temples and Agrigento

Head to Agrigento to visit the Valley of the Temples, a UNESCO World Heritage site with well-preserved ancient Greek temples.

Explore the archaeological museum to learn more about the history of the area. In the evening, enjoy the local cuisine, perhaps trying dishes like pasta con le sarde or arancini.

Day 4: The Baroque Towns of the Southeast

Visit the towns of the Sicilian Baroque, such as Ragusa, Modica, and Noto, known for their distinctive architecture. In Modica, taste the famous chocolate, known for its ancient Aztec recipe. Enjoy the beaches along the southeastern coast, like those near Marina di Ragusa.

Day 5: Mount Etna and Taormina

Explore Mount Etna, Europe's largest active volcano. You can take a guided tour or hike along some of the trails. In the afternoon, visit Taormina, a hilltop town with a famous Greek theater and stunning views of the Ionian Sea. Stroll along Corso Umberto, Taormina's main street, and enjoy the town's chic boutiques and cafes.

Day 6: The Aeolian Islands

Take a day trip to the Aeolian Islands, a UNESCO World Heritage site. You can visit islands like Lipari, Vulcano, or Stromboli, each with its unique charm and attractions. Enjoy activities like swimming in crystal-clear waters, hiking, or visiting archaeological sites.

Day 7: Departure from Catania

Spend your last day in Catania, Sicily's second-largest city, known for its Baroque architecture and vibrant fish market. Visit the Catania Cathedral and the Ursino Castle, and enjoy a stroll along Via Etnea. Depart from Catania's international airport.

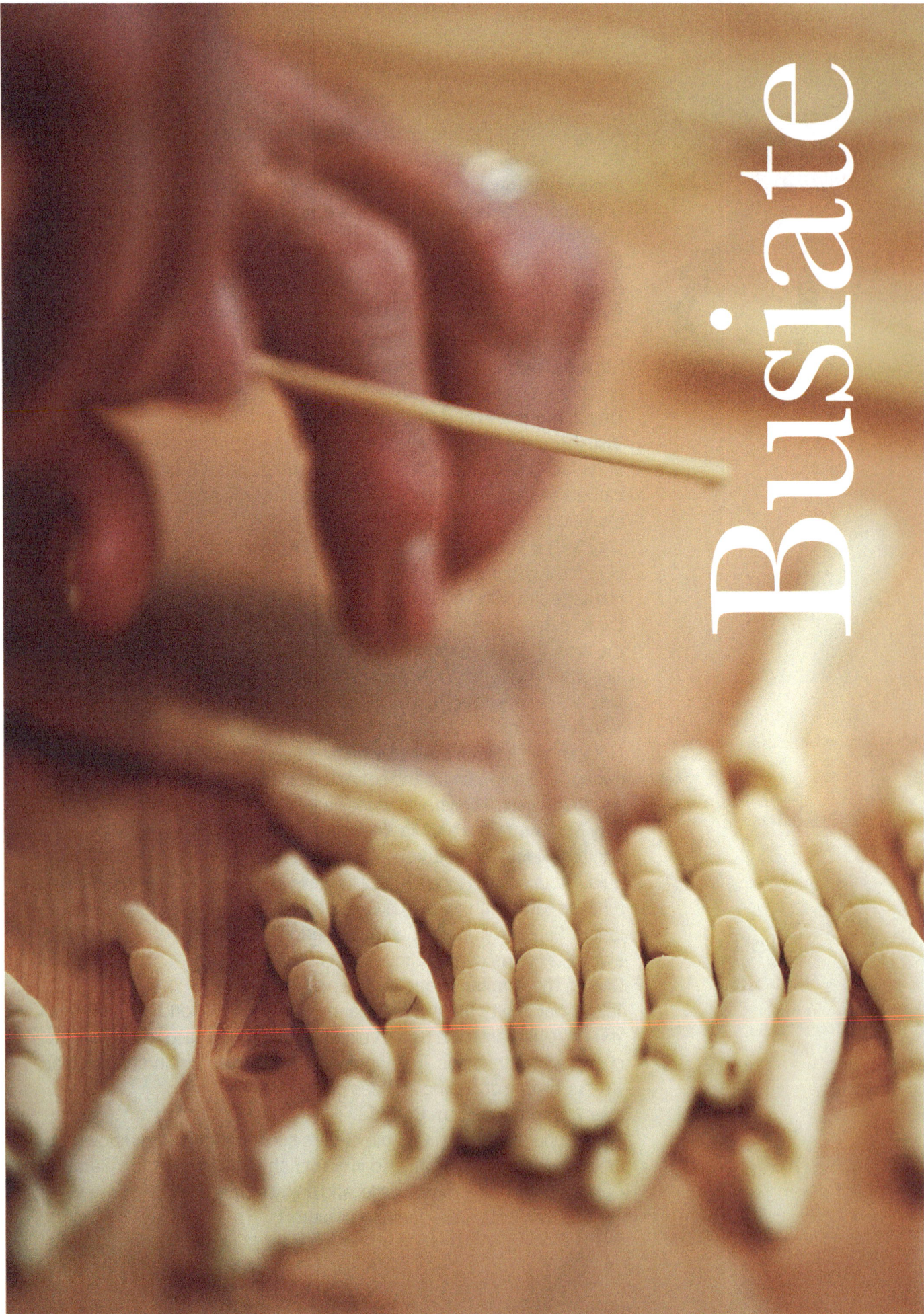

Busiate

Homemade pasta from Sicily

Homemade pasta from Sicily, an island rich in culinary history influenced by various cultures, reflects a unique blend of flavors and traditions. Sicilian pasta is known for its diverse shapes and regional specialties. Here are some key types of pasta and dishes typical of Sicily:

Busiate: Traditional twisted pasta from the Trapani region, often made by wrapping the dough around a thin rod or twig. Busiate is typically served with Trapanese pesto, made from tomatoes, almonds, garlic, basil, and pecorino cheese.

Cavateddi: A type of pasta from the area around Ragusa and Siracusa, resembling small cavatelli. They are often served with simple, hearty sauces like a pork ragù.

Anelletti: Small ring-shaped pasta, famously used in "Anelletti al Forno," a baked pasta dish that includes meat sauce, peas, and often topped with a béchamel sauce and mozzarella or caciocavallo cheese.

Maccaruna: A traditional pasta from the region of Messina, these are long, thick, hand-rolled noodles, similar to maccheroni. They are typically served with a rich meat sauce or in a soup.

Busiate al Pesto Trapanese

Busiate with Trapanese Pesto

Ingredients

For the Busiate:
400 gr. of durum wheat semolina flour
200 ml of water (approximately)
A pinch of salt

For the Pesto Trapanese:
300 gr of ripe tomatoes, peeled and deseeded
100 gr of blanched almonds
2 cloves of garlic
50 gr of grated Pecorino cheese
(or a mix of Pecorino and Parmesan)
A handful of fresh basil leaves
100 ml of extra virgin olive oil
Salt and pepper (to taste)

Instructions

Making the Busiate:
In a large bowl, mix the semolina flour and salt.
Gradually add water, kneading until a smooth dough forms.
Let the dough rest for about 30 minutes.

Forming Busiate:
Take small pieces of dough and roll them into long, thin ropes. Wrap each rope around a knitting needle or similar rod to create a spiral shape. Slide off to form the busiate. Cook the busiate in boiling salted water until they are al dente.

Preparing the Pesto Trapanese:
In a food processor or blender, combine the tomatoes, almonds, garlic, cheese, and basil. Blend until smooth. Gradually add the olive oil while blending, until the pesto reaches a creamy consistency. Season with salt and pepper to taste. Once the busiate is cooked, drain it, reserving some pasta water. Toss the busiate with the pesto Trapanese,
adding a little pasta water if needed to loosen the pesto. Plate the Busiate al Pesto Trapanese, garnishing with additional cheese or basil leaves if desired.

Maccaruna, Mandorle e Gamberi di Lipari
Maccaruna, Almonds, and Shrimps from Lipari

Ingredients

For the Maccaruna:
400 gr of durum wheat semolina flour
200 ml of water (approximately)
A pinch of salt

For the Sauce:
400 gr of shrimp (Lipari or similar quality), peeled and deveined
100 gr of almonds (preferably from Lipari), coarsely chopped
50 ml of olive oil
2 cloves of garlic, minced
1 small red chili pepper, finely chopped (optional for heat)
Salt and pepper (to taste)
A handful of fresh parsley, chopped
Zest of 1 lemon

Instructions

Making the Maccaruna:
In a large bowl, mix the semolina flour and salt. Gradually add water, kneading until a firm, smooth dough forms.
Rest the Dough: Let the dough rest, covered, for about 30 minutes.

Forming Maccaruna:
Roll small pieces of dough into long, thin ropes.
Cut them into desired lengths to form maccaruna. Cook the maccaruna in boiling salted water until they are al dente.

Preparing the Sauce:
In a dry skillet, toast the almonds until golden brown.
Set aside. In the same skillet, heat olive oil.
Add the garlic and chili pepper. Add the shrimp and sauté until they turn pink and are cooked through. Season with salt, pepper, and lemon zest.
Stir in the parsley and toasted almonds.
Drain the maccaruna, reserving some pasta water.
Add the pasta to the skillet with the shrimp. Toss to combine, adding a bit of pasta water if needed to loosen the sauce.

Busiate alla Norma
Busiate Norma-Style

Ingredients
For the Busiate:
400 gr of durum wheat semolina flour
200 ml of water (approximately)
A pinch of salt
For the Alla Norma Sauce:
2 medium eggplants, diced
Salt (for draining eggplant and to taste)
400 gr of crushed tomatoes
50 ml of olive oil
1 onion, finely chopped
2 cloves of garlic, minced
Fresh basil leaves
150 gr of ricotta salata cheese, grated or shaved
Pepper (to taste)
Olive oil (for frying eggplant)

Instructions
Making the Busiate:
In a bowl, mix the semolina flour and salt. Gradually add water, kneading until a firm, smooth dough forms.
Let it rest for about 30 minutes.
Forming Busiate:
Roll small pieces of dough into long, thin ropes.
Wrap each rope around a knitting needle or similar rod to create a spiral shape. Slide off to form busiate. Cook the busiate in boiling salted water until they are al dente.
Preparing the Alla Norma Sauce:
Sprinkle the diced eggplant with salt and let it sit in a colander for about 30 minutes to drain the bitter juices. Rinse and pat dry. Heat olive oil in a pan and fry the eggplant pieces until golden brown. Remove and set aside on paper towels. In the same pan, add more olive oil if needed. Sauté the onion and garlic until soft. Add the crushed tomatoes to the pan.
Season with salt and pepper. Let the sauce simmer for about 15-20 minutes.
Add the fried eggplant and torn basil leaves.
Drain the busiate and add them to the sauce. Toss to coat the pasta evenly. Sprinkle the grated or shaved ricotta salata cheese over the pasta. Plate the Busiate alla Norma, garnishing with additional basil leaves or more cheese if desired.

I hope I have created
a book that you liked.
If so, I ask you to leave
a review to help other
readers choose.

Thank you,
Stefano

Made in the USA
Las Vegas, NV
03 July 2024

91833312R00142